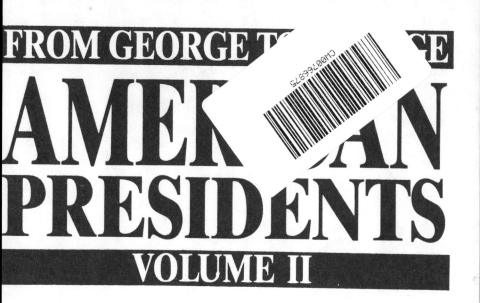

FROM GEORGE TO ~~GEORGE~~

AMERICAN PRESIDENTS

VOLUME II

by

RICHARD L. McELROY

Illustrations by Walt Neal

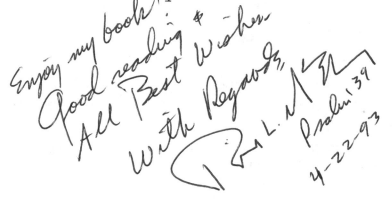

Enjoy my book!
Good reading &
All Best Wishes
With Regards,
Rich L. McElroy
Psalm 39
4-22-93

DARING PUBLISHING GROUP, INC.

DARING BOOKS • LIFE ENRICHMENT PUBLISHERS
CANTON • OHIO

For further information, write
Daring Books
913 Tuscarawas St., West
Canton, Ohio 44702

Cover design by Rich Hendrus

Library of Congress Cataloging-in-Publication Data
(Revised for vol. 2)

McElroy, Richard L., 1947-

American presidents.

Includes bibliographical references.
Contents: v. 1. Fascinating facts, stories & questions of our chief
executives and their families -- v. 2. From George to George.
1. Presidents--United States--Miscellanea.
2. United States--Politics and government--Miscellanea.   I. Title.
E176.1.M426   1984   973'.09'92   84-9606
ISBN 0-93893-618-2 (v. 1 : pbk.)
ISBN 1-878302-04 3 (v. 2)

Dedication

This book is dedicated to that rarest of human species — a friend. Tom Hayes, of Canton, has served as a critic and confidant. Without his help, this book would not have been possible.

Table of Contents

Acknowledgements

I owe a debt of gratitude to a number of fine people. Many thanks go to Larry Moesle and John Dahler of Canton who were instrumental in organizing my material. Other Canton residents providing assistance include Paul Keller, Jim Eakin, Carol Neiss, Rev. Douglas Patton, Doris Imboden, and Wilson Rownd. The following individuals also provided help in my research: Editor Mike Hanke and Gary Brown of the *Canton Repository*, Larry Pollack of Columbus, Mike Bricker of Orrville, and Professor of History George Knepper at the University of Akron. In addition, the fine staffs of the Stark County Historical Society and public library of Bellaire, Michigan were helpful. Last, but not least, I wish to thank my wife, Pam, and our three children, Matt, Rachael, and Luke for their patience and understanding the past five years.

Introduction

Americans are inveterate president watchers. Lacking kings and queens, dukes and duchesses, we satisfy our need for vicarious excitement by hanging on every word and deed of our Presidents. We automatically attribute celebrity status to them, ranking them alongside sports, music and entertainment figures as persons whose every move is news.

Presidents are the nation's most enduring celebrities. They die, but they don't "fade away." What they did and what they said lives on. As Teddy Roosevelt remarked, the presidency is a "bully pulpit," and those who have occupied that pulpit have left an enduring impression.

Presidential reputations change over time. George Washington was the only man to enter upon his duties with near unanimous support and approval. But even the "Father of his country" became subject to vicious attacks before he had completed his two terms. Nevertheless, his achievement was so extraordinary (and the attacks on his character so meanly motivated by political jealousy) that he has stood unchallenged since his own time as perhaps our greatest president. Some presidents, such as Lincoln and Truman, had severe critics in their own time but now enjoy high marks from the experts. Others, like Kennedy, were widely lauded at the conclusion of their tenure but suffered a diminished reputation over time.

In our constant search for political wisdom and guidance, we haul out and reexamine the words and deeds of past presidents. Even some of our less successful presidents contributed words which seem worthy of respect. They take on luster over the years. We tend to exaggerate the virtues of former presidents and to forgive them their trespasses. In the process we tend to sanctify them and, to the extent that we succeed, we lose sight of their human traits.

This book helps us recapture that elusive humanity. Foibles are revealed; triumphs are celebrated. We note that many of our presidents were rather ordinary men, and it is well that we remember this, for it is a healthy antidote to our hero-worshipping proclivities.

One sure way to put presidents in the main stream of human experience is to learn about their families; the relationships they had with wives and children. Politically and socially active wives such as Eleanor Roosevelt and Rosalyn Carter were much in the public eye. Wives such as Mamie Eisenhower and Bess Truman preferred to remain in the background. Lincoln and FDR had to endure criticism because of the way their sons were handled by the military. Lincoln's son Tad disrupted cabinet meetings; Alice Roosevelt smoked in public to the horror of moralists; the Ford children were criticized for indulging in questionable practices which were part of the folkways of their generation, and so it goes. Presidential brothers have been a special cross, witness Billy Carter, Sam Houston Johnson and Donald Nixon. Even presidential dogs — Lyndon Johnson's beagle and FDR's Fala — can be used by those wanting to embarrass the chief executive.

Presidents are expected to be regular fellows whether kissing babies; wearing Indian war bonnets; or tossing out the first baseball. Yet we also expect them to retain their dignity; to meet the potentates and rulers of the world on an equal footing; and to engender respect for the office and the nations. We force them to make absurd promises while campaigning; then we chastise them for failing to deliver once in office. We expect our president to be tough enough to work in the political jungles; yet we are shocked when we learn that he used the earthy language common to those precincts, or that he is capable of a vendetta against political enemies.

The presidency is full of contradictions: it is glamorous and mundane; it sets agendas but can accomplish little without Congress; it appoints postmasters in tiny crossroad villages and negotiates treaties with superpowers. And the men, (or, in the future, women) who must cope with these incredible complexities are not supermen living on a higher plane than the rest of humanity. The virtue of this book is to remind us of this.

Richard McElroy is well qualified to serve as our guide through this absorbing material. He is an experienced history teacher and publisher. Service as a city councilman has given him a feel for grass roots politics and an empathy for those who labor in the political realm. You will find his book entertaining, reassuring and instructive.

George W. Knepper
The University of Akron

Presidents of the United States

President	Place and Year of Birth	
1. George Washington	Virginia	1732
2. John Adams	Massachusetts	1735
3. Thomas Jefferson	Virginia	1743
4. James Madison	Virginia	1751
5. James Monroe	Virginia	1758
6. John Quincy Adams	Massachusetts	1767
7. Andrew Jackson	South Carolina	1767
8. Martin Van Buren	New York	1782
9. William Henry Harrison	Virginia	1773
10. John Tyler	Virginia	1790
11. James K. Polk	North Carolina	1795
12. Zachary Taylor	Virginia	1784
13. Millard Fillmore	New York	1800
14. Franklin Pierce	New Hampshire	1804
15. James Buchanan	Pennsylvania	1791
16. Abraham Lincoln	Kentucky	1809
17. Andrew Johnson	North Carolina	1808
18. Ulysses S. Grant	Ohio	1822
19. Rutherford B. Hayes	Ohio	1822
20. James A. Garfield	Ohio	1831
21. Chester A. Arthur	Vermont	1829
22. Grover Cleveland	New Jersey	1837
23. Benjamin Harrison	Ohio	1833
24. Grover Cleveland	New Jersey	1837
25. William McKinley	Ohio	1843
26. Theodore Roosevelt	New York	1858
27. William Howard Taft	Ohio	1857
28. Woodrow Wilson	Virginia	1856
29. Warren G. Harding	Ohio	1865
30. Calvin Coolidge	Vermont	1872
31. Herbert Hoover	Iowa	1874
32. Franklin D. Roosevelt	New York	1882
33. Harry S Truman	Missouri	1884
34. Dwight D. Eisenhower	Texas	1890
35. John F. Kennedy	Massachusetts	1917
36. Lyndon B. Johnson	Texas	1908
37. Richard M. Nixon	California	1913
38. Gerald R. Ford	Nebraska	1913
39. Jimmy Carter	Georgia	1924
40. Ronald Reagan	Illinois	1911
41. George Bush	Massachusetts	1922

Quiz Time

Answers begin on page 124.

1. Which President, prior to being sworn in, gave an order that the new Vice President was not to speak in public?

2. Which President once served as Provisional Governor of Cuba?

3. Which President defeated a well-known weightlifter in an arm-wrestling contest?

4. The twenty-dollar bill had to be redesigned after Harry Truman became President. Why?

5. Comedian Rodney Dangerfield, who gets "no respect," posed in *People* magazine with a pigeon on his head. Dangerfield said the pigeon mistook him for a statue of a U.S. President. To which Chief Executive was the comedian referring?

6. This President's football career was cut short when he hurt his leg trying to tackle legendary Jim Thorpe in a college game. Name him.

7. Who was the first President-elect to enter Washington D.C. by train?

8. Socialist leader Norman Thomas ran unsuccessfully for President four times. As a boy, he worked for a future President. Which one?

9. The Presidency of the United States was the only political office this man ever held. Name him.

10. This President told his personal lawyer, "Last night I went to sleep and hoped I'd never wake up." Name him.

11. Which President often read three books in an evening?

12. This President, a published poet, wore the same hat for ten years. Name him.

13. Thomas Jefferson once referred to this future Chief Executive as a "dangerous man." Name him.

14. Which President proposed to his wife the first day he met her?

15. Which President pitched horseshoes with friends on the White House lawn?

16. As a youngster, this future President was walking along a wilderness trail when he encountered Johnny Appleseed and given a polished apple and a bag of seeds. Who was he?

17. Henry Hudson explored North America in the 16th Century in his ship, *Half Moon*. But a smaller vessel of the same name was the favorite ship of which future President?

18. Which 19th Century President had 400,000 more votes in his second election but lost?

19. Which President persuaded Henry Ford to run for the U.S. Senate, only to see him lose?

20. Who was the first union president to become President of the United States?

21. This man has been described as the "Father of the American Mule" because he developed that breed of animal by successfully crossing a donkey and a horse. Before becoming President he was often referred to as the "Jackass Matchmaker." Name him.

22. Which noted American told Calvin Coolidge that he was sleeping too much?

23. Which President was married by a Catholic priest even though he and his bride were Protestants?

24. Which President was named *twice* after his father?

25. Teddy Roosevelt was once a deputy sheriff in which state?

26. This President had a deformed finger, nearly losing it as a young man when he got it caught in a cotton gin. Name him.

27. Name the future Chief Executive who worked 15-hour days as a college president, but accepted no salary.

28. John Adams and Thomas Jefferson both died on July 4, 1826. Can you name the only other President to die on July 4th?

29. Who was the only President to receive part of his education in Poland?

30. As of 1992, how many cabinet members served the President?

31. As a Congressman, this future President distinguished himself when he refused to vote in favor of sending a letter of thanks to George Washington on his retirement from the Presidency. Name him.

32. As a teenage lifesaver, this future President saved 77 swimmers from drowning. Name him.

33. Which President initiated the Medal of Freedom, the nation's highest civilian award?

34. Name one of two future Presidents married in London.

35. This President had the first elevator installed in the White House because of health problems. Name him.

36. This man's last job prior to becoming President was that of a clerk in a common pleas court. Name him.

37. At the Treaty of Versailles ending World War I, what territory did President Wilson request and receive?

38. Which man defeated the first Catholic candidate, the first woman candidate, and the first black Vice Presidential candidate?

39. Which 20th Century President always slept with a loaded pistol under his pillow?

40. Which President wore gloves while fishing and always had a Secret Service agent bait his hook?

41. Who was the first incumbent President to challenge his opponent to a debate?

42. Who was the President when America commissioned her first admiral?

43. Name the President who won a smashing victory, capturing 49 states after he voted on Election Day in Solvang, California.

44. Can you name the 19th Century President who had little more than a cup of coffee for breakfast?

45. Who was President when the first child was born in the White House?

46. If and when a married woman becomes President of the United States, her husband (according to protocol) shall be referred to as what?

47. There is only one American Presidential landmark operated by the National Park Service *outside* the boundaries of the United States. Names either the place, or the President involved.

48. This future President witnessed the Battle of Bunker Hill with his mother. Name him.

49. Which President's father was a college classmate of Thomas Jefferson?

50. Which city has been the site of the most Presidential conventions?

51. Which President killed a bat with his saber to protect his wife?

52. After asking Congress to declare war, this President ordered U.S. forces to attack Canada. Name him.

53. Which numbered box was President Lincoln sitting in when he was shot at Ford's Theater?

54. Warren G. Harding invented two words which have become part of the English language. One of these words was "normalcy." What was the other word?

55. Which future President was a centerfielder for Davidson College, but failed to make the varsity baseball team when he transferred to another school?

56. What was so unusual about celebrity Ronald Reagan's 1955 appearance on the television show "I've Got a Secret"?

57. Whose portrait is on the $50 U.S. Savings Bond?

58. Which President attended an inauguration wearing only one shoe?

59. As a boy, this President nearly drowned four times in a six-week period. Name him.

60. This candidate, while campaigning in the Midwest, stopped at a day care center and told young children he was special because he could "talk to fish." Name him.

61. U. S. Presidents Van Buren, Grant, Arthur, Cleveland, Coolidge, Hoover, Eisenhower, Carter and Bush all had different political backgrounds, but all of them indulged in this favorite hobby. What was it?

62. This President had the longest distance phone call to another individual. Name the Chief Executive.

63. Which President wrote the first airmail letter?

64. Name the only man who had a *grandmother* living when he was elected President.

65. In Secret Service and Presidential terminology, what is the "football"?

66. Can you name one of the two Presidents who were nominated by their party in a church?

67. "Scamp" was the name of which President's dog?

68. Which 19th Century Presidential candidate ran unopposed?

69. Which President, during his college days, was nicknamed the "Kansas Cyclone"?

70. Who was the first President to file an income tax return?

71. Who was the first President since John Adams to address a joint session of Congress?

72. Which retired President's yearly license plates always read 5-7-45?

73. Who is the only President to have the first name of Francis?

74. Thomas Jefferson, James Monroe, and John Tyler were all graduates of this eastern university. Name it.

75. Which President was sworn into office by his father?

76. Which 20th Century President announced, "I find that up here on top of a mountain it is easier for me to get on top of the job"?

77. Which President had "Happy Birthday" sung to him by the entire House and Senate?

78. Other than James A. Garfield, who was the only other ordained minister to become President?

79. Which U.S. President announced his opposition to the use of Christmas trees?

80. Famed artist Gilbert Stuart intended to paint a full portrait of this President, but painted only his head. Name the President.

81. Name the 20th Century President who appointed a great-grandson of a President as Secretary of the Navy.

82. In his first message to Congress, this President promised to serve a single term. He broke his promise, however, and ran again successfully. Name him.

83. Name the future President who was once a forest ranger in Yellowstone National Park.

84. Who was the first President to have his voice mechanically recorded?

85. Who was the first deceased President to lie in state in the U.S. Capitol rotunda?

86. Louie Howe often told this President to "go to hell" and still remained an intimate friend. Name the President.

87. Which President has left the country with the most direct descendants?

88. Which President, along with his Vice President, dedicated the cornerstone of the Smithsonian Institution?

89. Who was known as Ronald Reagan's "Iron Man"?

90. This President addressed a jury to make closing remarks when he was only 15 years old! Name him.

91. Which President's birthday became Navy Day?

92. Who was the first President NOT to attend the inauguration of his successor?

93. The parents of this future President had three family Bibles, one Greek, one

German, and one King James version. Name this family.

94. In the event a President is impeached, what roles do the House of Representatives, the U.S. Senate, and the Chief Justice of the Supreme Court serve?

95. Upon this President's passing, Mormon leader Brigham Young declared that he "is dead and gone to hell, and I'm glad of it!" Name the President to whom Young was referring.

96. Which future President, after returning from nearly two years of war, was thrown out of his house by his grandmother?

97. Three Presidents, all from the same state, successfully conducted "front porch" campaigns where the people came to them. Name two of these three men.

98. Which administration was dubbed the "Mom and Pop Presidency"?

99. Which President was a graduate of Dickinson College in Carlisle, Pennsylvania?

100. Which President was Godfather to the Duke of Kent, the youngest brother of King George VI?

101. Which President collapsed in Pueblo, Colorado, while on a speaking tour?

102. This President's father-in-law cursed him, called him a "nigger" and refused to attend the wedding. Name him.

103. As a youngster, this President was nicknamed "Little Mat" by his parents. Name him.

104. Which President's grandson covered major league baseball games as a columnist?

105. Name the nineteenth century President who established the first overseas consulate with Japan.

106. Who was the first President to have his picture taken during his inaugural address?

107. At this President's inauguration, a band of Chippewa Indians, who had once been defeated by the new President danced for hours in his honor. Name him.

20

108. *Air Force One* is the name of the President's jet airliner. But what is the name of his personal helicopter?

109. Flags mistakenly flew at half mast for this President a day *before* he died. Name him.

110. Which President, so embittered with news media, banned television cameras from his last two press conferences, and vowed to continue that policy if reelected?

111. This future President, while addressing his fellow Congressmen in the U.S. House of Representatives, was shouted at by Senator Henry Clay, "Go home, God damn you. Go home where you belong." Name him.

112. Most Americans know that Ronald Reagan was a movie and television star. In one of his most memorable films, he played a submarine commander, Casey Abbott, in "Hellcats of the Navy." Can you name the submarine he commanded?

113. George Washington was the only man ever to receive all electoral votes. But one other candidate received all but one. Can you name him?

114. Who was the first President to fly overseas?

115. Who was the last President born before the American Revolution?

116. Which President publicly referred to Thomas Edison as "America's greatest possession"?

117. Only two Presidents were survived by their father. Kennedy was one. Who was the other?

118. Talk about obscurity — name the President whose cabinet members included the following men: Lyman Gage (Treasury), Joseph McKenna (Attorney General), John Long (Navy), James Wilson (Agriculture), Cornelius Bliss (Interior), James Gary (Postmaster General), and Russell Alger (Secretary of War).

119. Which President's father was nicknamed "Peanuts" for his diminutive size?

120. Which President created the cabinet post of Secretary of the Interior (first called Secretary of the Home Department)?

121. Name the Presidential and Vice Presidential candidates who were both generals and who both became President.

122. This President, when he ran a second time, exclaimed, "There are so many people in this country who don't like me." Name him.

123. Prior to becoming President, this man served as ambassador to Great Britain, Holland, Prussia (Germany) and Russia, negotiated the Treaty of Ghent to end the War of 1812, and wrote the Monroe Doctrine. Name him.

124. Close friends and associates once told this future President, "You've got to stop talking all the time. You're a great guy, but you're boring people to death." Name the person so advised.

125. Name the only candidate to run for Vice President on a losing ticket and later become President?

126. Which President's daughter christened the battleship *U.S.S. Missouri*?

127. How many states are named after U.S. Presidents?

128. This future President practiced his flying lessons at the dinner table, using his silverware as controls. Name him.

129. Ohio-born Lillian and Dorothy Gish, both of whom were legendary film stars, claim to be related to which U.S. President?

130. In 1950, two Presidents were elected into the Hall of Fame of Great Americans, both of whom also won a Nobel Peace Prize. Name one of them.

131. Has a convention ever failed to nominate a man for President?

132. Which President had younger brother and sister twins named Randolph and Anna?

133. Which President, while attending college, broke into the Dean's office to find out his class ranking only to discover that he was first in his class?

134. This future President's life was saved when, during a surprise attack on his forces, he couldn't find his horse. Name him.

135. Which President graduated first or second in his college class of two students?

136. One of our Presidents had a namesake who became a great champion boxer. Name either the President or the boxer who was named in honor of the Chief Executive.

137. Which President was wounded four times in battle?

138. On the day this future President was born, his father remarked, "We have another General Grant at our house." Name him.

139. In Charles Dickens's only visit to the United States, he was greeted by which President?

140. What future President was known as the "Pious Moonlight Dude" while dating his wife-to-be in college?

141. Davy Crockett accused this President of being "laced up in corsets, such as women in town wear," and that he "struts and swaggers like a crow ..." To which Chief Executive was Crockett referring?

142. Who was the first President depicted on a U.S. coin (other than a commemorative one)?

143. Which President's father died while attempting to save a man from drowning?

144. As an eighth grader this future President informed his teacher he wanted to be like Lou Gehrig. Name him.

145. Which future President played the female role of Desdemona in Shakespeare's play "Othello"?

146. Which President formed a bucket brigade and fought for hours to extinguish flames at the Capitol Building?

147. Who was the first President to receive a woman ambassador from a foreign country?

148. Can you name the Chief Justice of the Supreme Court who swore in seven different Presidents?

149. Who succeeded Thomas Jefferson as rector (president and board chairman) of the University of Virginia?

150. Name either the first or last "dark horse" candidates to become President.

151. *New Republic* magazine described this President's new cabinet as consisting of "eight millionaires and one plumber." Name the President.

152. Which 20th Century President spent more than five years in the White House, but only attended three major league baseball games?

153. The first two Presidents to serve only one term had something in common. What was it?

154. How can you be certain that the President will read your letter to him?

155. Which President's son was nicknamed the "Prince of Nails" because of his elegant style, courtly manner, and Harvard education?

156. Which President superstitiously bowled an orange down the aisle of *Air Force One* before it took off?

157. Which President's pet became the first dog commissioned a private in the U.S. Army?

158. Which President appointed the most Supreme Court Justices?

159. When Andrew Jackson completed building his mansion *The Hermitage*, the very first guest he invited was a former U.S. President. Name him.

160. Which future President turned down offers to play pro football for the Green Bay Packers and the Detroit Lions?

161. Who was the first President to broadcast from outer space?

162. Washington Irving described this President as "the greatest and most available man" he had ever met. Talleyrand, the legendary French statesman, found this same American "superior, as a man of the world, to those of his compatriots I have seen until now." But William Seward of New York and others described this man as a "crawling reptile." Name the President to whom these people were referring.

163. At Runneymede, England, west of London, stands a memorial dedicated to King John who signed the Magna Carta (with an X) in 1215. But which American President is also memorialized there?

164. Three of our Presidents constantly suffered from chronic migraine headaches. Name two of them.

165. Which President was a college classmate of author Nathaniel Hawthorne, who wrote *The House of Seven Gables* and *The Scarlet Letter*?

166. As an ornery youth, this Chief Executive was spanked on numerous occasions by his father for such things as stealing a penny from the church offering and shooting his sister with a BB gun. Name him.

167. Only two Americans were elected President without campaigning for the office. George Washington was one. Who was the other?

168. Name the man who, before becoming President, had never voted and owned more than 300 slaves.

169. Which President mistakenly announced to the press that he was running "for the Governor of the United States"?

170. Which President's Secretary of the Treasury became his son-in-law?

171. Who was "the greatest man in the world," according to Thomas Jefferson?

172. Which President on the last day of his term helped his grandchild build a snowman outside the White House?

173. After winning the election in 1960, John Kennedy remarked that "we wouldn't have had a prayer without *that* gadget." To what was Kennedy referring?

174. Which President, while a cadet at West Point, rode a horse over a 6'6" hurdle, establishing a new record?

175. This future President played shortstop on his college baseball team as a freshman before a finger injury ended his career. Name him.

176. Which President's daughter held a party in a tree house designed by her father?

177. This Chief Executive was correct when he observed, "Oftentimes, as I sit here, I don't seem to grasp that I am President." Name him.

178. Which President is associated with one of the world's most famous palindromes (a quotation or verse which reads the same forward or backward)?

179. A college yearbook satirized this future President as a "Mexican athlete — good at throwing bull." Name him.

180. Which future President, while serving as military leader, won smashing victories over the enemy at the battles of Emuckfaw, Enotachopo, and Horseshoe Bend?

181. Which President issued a dress code to members of the Congress attending his inauguration?

182. Under which President was the Chief Justice of the Supreme Court also serving as a Secretary of State?

183. One President accused another of exercising psychic powers of "manipulation and deception," further adding, "He is seeking to make his followers 'Holy Rollers.'" Name one or both of the Presidents involved.

184. Which President officially recognized Thanksgiving as a national day of "praise and prayer . . . for the wonderful things He (God) has done in the Nation's behalf . . ."?

185. Who was the only U.S. President to witness a baseball triple play from a seat in the ball park?

186. This 20th Century President took his oath of office at the White House, not the Capitol. He also ordered no celebration following his inauguration. Name him.

187. Which President once worked as a special correspondent for International News Service?

188. Which President wrote and published a book *This Country of Ours* in the last years of his life?

189. Which leader was affectionately called "Santo" (Saint) by his people?

190. Which Chief Executive died just one week after conducting his 998th press conference?

191. All of us have heroes. Warren G. Harding was no exception. Which legendary American was Harding's hero?

192. When Gerald Ford took over the reins of the government following Nixon's resignation, he asked the Marine Band *not* to play "Hail to the Chief" or "Ruffles and Flourishes." Which song did he request?

193. Which President was shot while visiting "Rainbow City"?

194. Who was the first person FDR told that he would seek a fourth term as President?

195. In 1774, how long did it take John Adams to travel from Philadelphia to his home in Braintree, Massachusetts?

196. Which well-known public figure once said, "Ronald Reagan has had more influence on my life than any other man has"?

197. Which President lived in a palace called "The House of the Most High" surrounded by palm trees?

198. Which President was often addressed as "Foo-Foo Head" by his son?

199. Which President did poet Carl Sandburg refer to as "not a perfect man and yet more precious than fine gold"?

200. Which President was considered a wine connoisseur, once sampling and correctly identifying eleven of fourteen Madeira wines?

Matching

Answers begin on page 137.

Match the following Chief Executives with their nicknames.

A. Red Fox   1. James Garfield

B. Teacher President   2. Theodore Roosevelt

C. Surveyor President   3. George Washington

D. Mistletoe Politician   4. Franklin D. Roosevelt

E. Sphinx   5. Martin Van Buren

F. President De Facto   6. Thomas Jefferson

G. Four Eyes   7. Rutherford B. Hayes

Match the following Presidents with their yachts.

A. Dolphin   1. John F. Kennedy

B. Despatch   2. William McKinley

C. Sylph   3. Theodore Roosevelt
                                       and William Taft

D. Honey Fitz   4. Rutherford B. Hayes

Last Words. Match the following Presidents with the last words they spoke before they died.

A. "It is well."   1. Franklin D. Roosevelt

B. "Water."   2. James Madison

C. "I always talk better lying down."   3. George Washington

D. "Please put out the light."   4. Theodore Roosevelt

E. "I have a terrific headache."   5. Ulysses S. Grant

F. "America."   6. James Monroe

More nicknames.

A. Little Wizard   1. Andrew Johnson

B. The American Oak   2. James Monroe

C. The Preacher President   3. Herbert Hoover

D. Rugged Individualist   4. Martin Van Buren

E. Tennessee Tailor   5. Abraham Lincoln

F. Last of the Cocked Hats   6. James Garfield

G. Father of the American Dollar   7. Thomas Jefferson

Match the Presidential Portrait with the clues in the column on the right.

 A

1. He resigned from his post as Assistant Secretary of the Navy to lead men in a war against Spain.

 B

2. After failing to gain a Vice Presidential nomination, he then lost a U.S. Senate race in 1858.

 C

3. Artillery commander in World War I, he was a keen student of history and politics.

 D

4. A poor speller who never finished school, he owned slaves and thousands of acres of land.

 E

5. He had one of the country's best stamp collections and built model ships.

Presidents' Wives and First Ladies Only

Answers begin on page 138.

1. Which President's widow was the first to receive a pension?

2. Which First Lady said, "I don't like to take a chance on losing. I always want to win"?

3. Which First Lady, after one year in the White House, never entered the Green Room where her son was embalmed?

4. Name the former First Lady who received history's very first telegram and sent the first response.

5. Which First Lady was the youngest when she was married?

6. Which First Lady wore black during her entire stay in the White House?

7. Which future First Lady was called "Nell" by her father?

8. Name the only First Lady photographed in the nude.

9. Which First Lady met her future husband while they were attending geology classes in college?

10. Which First Lady put up the first Christmas tree in the White House?

11. Who was the first widow of a President to remarry?

12. This former First Lady died of severe burns when she fainted into a fireplace. Name her.

13. Which First Lady of the 1800's never saw the inside of the White House?

14. Which First Lady was nicknamed "Steel Magnolia" for her determination and frankness?

15. Which First Lady's cousin drew the design for the California state flag?

16. This First Lady told her husband after entering the White House, that "cigars are alright, but it's undignified to chew [tobacco]." Name her.

17. Which First Lady's childhood name was "Patsy," a name which her husband called her?

18. This President's wife, as an infant, was smuggled through enemy lines by her father who was disguised as a British redcoat. Name her.

19. A painting by which well-known artist hung above Mamie Eisenhower's White House bed?

20. This future First Lady was told by her fiance that he loved his country more than her. Name her.

21. Which First Lady refused to serve food at White House receptions?

22. Name the First Lady who demanded and got $35,000 from Congress to repair the White House, exterminate rats and bugs, lay new floors, paint and wallpaper walls, build new toilets and add electricity and plumbing.

23. "My husband left me yesterday morning" was written in a letter by which First Lady?

24. Which First Lady's carriage ran over a small boy while she was riding through the streets of Washington?

25. Name the only First Lady who eloped.

26. Which First Lady invited 200 guests to a White House dinner but, due to an error, had 500 persons arrive?

27. Which First Lady won two national awards at age eleven for her equestrian skills?

28. Which First Lady grew up in Rome?

29. This President's wife, after graduating *cum laude* from college, worked as a secretary, an x-ray technician, and played opposite her future husband in a theatrical play entitled *The Dark Tower*. Name her.

30. This 20th Century First Lady was once presented a $2.98 wedding ring, purchased at Sears and Roebuck by her husband. Name her.

First Lady Facts

Regarding her role as First Lady, Martha Washington said, "I am more like a state prisoner than anyone else."

Mamie Eisenhower moved into a hospital for eleven months — and she wasn't even sick. She did this in 1968 to stay with her ailing husband.

It was no problem for Grace Coolidge being married to "Silent Cal," the President who spoke very few words. For three years, she taught the deaf in Northampton, Massachusetts.

Lucy Hayes, wife of our nineteenth President, was the first to be called "The First Lady."

When Mary Lincoln was judged insane in 1872, she was immediately forced to surrender, from her underwear, $56,000 in government bonds!

Jackie Kennedy once referred to the Vice President and Mrs. Johnson as "Colonel Cornpone and his Little Pork Chop."

Rachel Jackson once exclaimed, " I would rather be a doorkeeper in the house of God, than live in that palace [White House]." The seventh President's wife died in December of 1828 just before Andrew left to assume the Presidency.

On June 13, 1985, there were more that one hundred birthday parties all for the same person! In Alexandria, Virginia and the Washington, D.C. area, businesses and institutions planned a birthday celebration for Martha Washington. The first First Lady was honored for her contributions to the founding of the nation.

Alice Roosevelt enjoyed entertaining visitors in her Washington D.C. home for many years. She once told friends that Calvin Coolidge looked "as if he had been weaned on a pickle."

Pat Nixon never smoked in public. In private, however, she was a chain smoker.

At the inaugural festivities in 1813, Dolley Madison served *her* favorite flavor of ice cream — strawberry.

George Bush lost "Barbara" four times during World War II. This was the name of each of his dive bombers he lost in training sessions and combat. Stationed on the aircraft *San Jacinto*, Bush's last mission saw him crash land in the sea. He lost his co-pilot and navigator, but was rescued by a submarine. He was awarded the Distinguished Flying Cross, returned home to enter college and married Barbara.

Though FDR and his wife were not always on the best of terms, they still had high regard and respect for one another. During World War II when the First Lady was out of the country, the President missed her. On one occasion when Eleanor was overseas, there was some discussion as to how she should travel home. FDR finally sent out an order: "I don't care how you send her home, just send her."

The formal etiquette by which the White House social affairs are conducted was established by President John Quincy Adams and his wife, Louisa, in 1825, and have remained in effect with few changes since.

Mary McElroy (no relation to the author) served as First Lady during part of Chester Arthur's term in office. She was the younger sister of the twenty-first President.

Martha Washington once described herself as on "old fashioned housekeeper . . . cheerful as a cricket."

Nancy Reagan's given names are Anne Francis (Robbins).

Mary Lincoln had a notorious reputation for buying extravagant clothing. The President's complaints about her sporadic shopping sprees did no good. The First Lady just laughed, and often told her husband, "I am determined my next husband *shall be rich.*" Some people regarded such remarks as sincere, but Mary Todd Lincoln had a deep, abiding love for Abraham.

Referring to his failure to be reelected President in 1980, Jimmy Carter said, "I'm not bitter, but Rosalynn is."

FDR once said of Eleanor, "Never get into an argument with the missus. You can't win."

In 1920, Florence Harding visited a well-known fortune teller in Washington, D.C. and was informed that her husband would be elected President, but that he would die in office.

While serving at the Executive Mansion in Philadelphia, Martha Washington was addressed as "Your Majesty" by visiting ladies attending receptions.

Andrew Johnson became President after Lincoln's assassination. Eliza Johnson, however, was too ill with tuberculosis to assume any official duties.

Therefore, the President's daughter, Martha, conducted the White House social activities. She quickly informed the public, "We are plain people from the hills of Tennessee, called here for a short time by a national calamity. I trust not too much will be expected of us."

Eleanor Roosevelt's plain features did not escape even the ridicule of her mother. The child was often referred to as "granny " and "ugly duckling." In addition, Mom scolded her daughter constantly for her clumsiness and disinterest in spelling.

Only one First Lady since Grace Coolidge has lit the large Christmas tree on the White House lawn — that was Nancy Reagan.

Upon retiring to Mount Vernon from the duties of Chief Executive, Martha Washington remarked, "The General and I feel like children just released from school."

Eleanor Roosevelt's German shepherd once bit the Prime Minister of Canada.

Mary Lincoln once overspent a Congressional allowance to redecorate the White House. Her husband was furious and told her, "It can never have my approval. I'll pay it out of my pocket first — it would stink in the nostrils of the American people to have it said the President of the United States had approved a bill over-running the appropriation of $20,000 for flub dubs for this damned old house, when the soldiers cannot have blankets."

Mamie Doud Eisenhower frequently spent afternoons playing canasta with a group of personal friends from her days as an Army wife. The press often referred to this group as "Mamie's Bridge Cabinet."

Lady Bird Johnson's advice on the best way to overcome shyness is "to become so wrapped up in something that you forget to be afraid."

It was a shock to President Grover Cleveland and his young wife, Frances, that the voters chose Benjamin Harrison as the next Chief Executive. Though discouraged of her husband's bid for reelection, Frances Folsom Cleveland told the servants as she left the White House, " I want you to take good care of the house . . . We are coming back just four years from today." And she was right.

Martha Washington was not being sarcastic when she wrote a relative, explaining about her husband, "George is right; he is always right." This quote was a response which characterized George's position against England as "folly."

Barbara Bush and her husband enjoyed their thirteen-month stay in the People's Republic of China. In mid-September of 1974, George Bush, former U.N. Ambassador, was appointed as U.S. envoy to China by President Ford. Moving overseas meant learning as much as possible about Chinese history and customs. Barbara prepared thoroughly for the venture, and when she was introduced to the Chinese Ambassador in Washington, Huang Zhen, she asked if they could take along their new pet cocker spaniel, C. Fred. Though dogs were not entirely acceptable in China under Mao Tse Tung's rule, Huang informed her that it would be all right to take the pooch. When the Bushes took C. Fred for walks, some Chinese seemed confused, pointing to the small animal and saying, "Moa!", the Chinese word for cat. And at a formal dinner one evening, Barbara and George ate an item listed on the menu as "fragrant meat." After returning home, a staff member familiar with Chinese customs explained that they had eaten "the upper lip of a wild dog."

More than a year before she married Major William McKinley, Ida Saxton and her sister were sent on a grand tour of Europe by their father in 1869. For several months, the girls visited historic sites in Ireland, Scotland, England, France, Germany, Italy and Switzerland. A highlight of their journey was a meeting with Pope Pius IX. Garbed in appropriate black veils and black dresses, they were presented to His Holiness after waiting quite some time. In a letter to their parents in Canton, Ohio, the young ladies, raised as strict Presbyterians, reassured them that though they had bowed and kissed his hand, they did so "not because he's Pope, but such a nice old man." In subsequent correspondence, Ida urged her parents not to let anyone else read her letters.

While attending Georgia Southwestern Junior College, Rosalynn Carter majored in interior decorating. No doubt this subject proved pragmatic in preparing her for duties as First Lady.

Martha Washington once cut up her husband's Continental Army uniform to make herself a satin handbag.

In the winter of 1777, ten-year-old John Quincy Adams told his mother, Abigail, "Mar, I never saw anybody so fat as you do." Mrs. Adams had good reason to be. At age 32, she was pregnant with her fifth child, a girl which was stillborn the following July.

It Happened Like This . . .

Bachelor Father?

Practically every schoolboy knows that James Buchanan was our only bachelor President. But what most people don't know concerns a gravestone in Canton, Ohio, at Rowland Cemetery on East Tuscarawas Street. A stone marker there is inscribed *M. Henrietta Buchanan. Died December 17, 1855. Age 41 years.* Beneath that marker lies the remains of what many believe to be the daughter of our fifteenth President. The mother is probably buried nearby, but many of the tombstones in the old cemetery are broken, misplaced and weather-worn. Though this story is not generally known outside of Canton, it has been a well-kept secret. Until now.

When the future President was 20 years old, he fell in love with a young Mennonite girl in Lancaster, Pennsylvania. Later, when she discovered she was pregnant, Buchanan made up his mind to marry her. His parents, Scotch-Irish Presbyterians did not wish to see their son's future impaired; at the time he was a lawyer and seeking a seat in the state legislature.

During this same period, Buchanan was courting Ann Coleman. She was the daughter of Lancaster County's wealthiest businessman, and they were about to announce their engagement when Miss Coleman called it off. Due to some vicious gossip which had reached her, she informed her suitor by letter that they could never marry. In December of 1819, she traveled east to Philadelphia. On the way, however, she died from an overdose of laudanum, an opium derivative. Though it was never proven, her death was an apparent suicide.

Also leaving town with no prior warning, the Mennonite girl headed west in a wagon. Buchanan traced her to Canton, Ohio, where she had stopped because she was ill. Some Mennonites who probably knew her family cared for her and helped raise her daughter. In the ensuing years, Buchanan learned more details and sent money to help provide relief. By the time the daughter reached adulthood, her mother had died. James Buchanan was already established in politics, having served in the U.S. Congress and as ambassador to Russia.

There have been numerous articles published about this incident, and the facts seem quite convincing. According to one account reprinted in 1982 by the Stark County Chapter of the Ohio Genealogical Society, many older Cantonians "remember the flowers that were placed on the grave of the mother and daughter by money set aside by President Buchanan during his life and through his will after his death, to keep fresh the graves of his child and the girl he loved."

James Buchanan was well-qualified for the Presidency, but proved to be an ineffectual leader as the country headed towards civil war. He was, however, a man of unimpeachable honesty and patriotism. It seems only proper that this sensitive man provide care and comfort for the woman he loved. And if indeed

39

he made a mistake as a young man, he bore that burden of guilt for the rest of his life.

Almost Saved From Marriage

A young soldier from Ohio received word that his girlfriend back home was keeping company with another man. The enraged private applied for a furlough, but it was refused. He deserted, went home, and married the girl. A short time later he was arrested, tried, and sentenced to be shot. Journalist Petroleum V. Nasby (David R. Locke), a favorite of the President, went to the White House and asked Lincoln to pardon the man. Lincoln gladly signed a pardon, then remarked to Locke, "I want to punish the young man — probably in less than a year he will wish I had withheld the pardon . . ."

Retaliation

One of the duties of the Secret Service is to protect the President and his family. Beginning in 1972, these federal police agents found it increasingly difficult to work at the White House with the Nixons. Several changes were instituted, and some of the Secret Service people did not like it. Pat Nixon, for instance, did not like to see men's hairy arms and soon an order came forth disallowing all Executive Protective Service employees to wear short-sleeve shirts. They were also ordered to wear their wool jackets while on duty. But in Washington it gets rather warm, and as the summer sun sizzled, so did some of the agents. Revenge came swiftly when agents began waking the President at random times after midnight. By clapping their hands or yelling, they scared the hundreds of birds perched in a tree just below Nixon's second-story bedroom near the South Portico. This commotion often caused Nixon to get up and turn on the light to see what the disturbance was. And the agents had to be careful to stay out of the range of security cameras outside of the White House. This "war" went on for several months, providing Nixon with interrupted sleep.

A Case for Libel?

Newspapers labeled President Lincoln in a number of uncomplimentary ways. The press referred to him as "Satan," "Baboon," "Ass," "Gorilla," "Dictator," "Barbarian," "Great Criminal," "awful ugly," and "serpentine." And these were *northern* newspapers, particularly ones in New York and Chicago.

Who was Vernon (as in Mount)?

Lawrence Washington, George's brother, renamed his Little Hunting Creek home in honor of Admiral Edward Vernon. Lawrence had served under

Vernon in 1739 when the English attacked the Spanish on the coast of Colombia. When he died, the estate went to his mother and younger brother, George.

Nerve Shattering

On September 5, 1901, President McKinley and his wife traveled to Buffalo, New York, where they were greeted with a twenty-one gun salute as their special train pulled into the station. The thunderous roar of the guns was too much for Mrs. McKinley, and she fainted.

Corrupted Youth

John Adams used tobacco (both chewing and smoking) for more that sixty years, even though he tried to give it up. Our second President first was introduced to the habit "upon the Ponds of Ice, when Skating with the Boys at Eight Years of Age."

A Kid at Heart

When Edith Roosevelt gave birth to her fourth son, Quentin, in November of 1897, she told friends, "Now I have *five* boys." The total, of course, included her husband, Theodore.

Brainless Senate

A New Jersey newspaperman once asked retired President Woodrow Wilson if he would consider running for the U.S. Senate, the legislative body which had rejected his League of Nations proposal. Wilson replied that the Senate wasn't worth "a damn" and that it hadn't had a thought there in "fifty years."

Parting Words

Sometimes we find it difficult to express ourselves, and often say the wrong thing at the wrong time. Immediately following Richard Nixon's resignation from the Presidency, he was leaving the White House to fly to his California home. On his way out, Betty Ford told him, "Have a nice trip."

Harding's Harsh Words

Scandals rocked the Harding Administration. The 29th President realized that many of his cronies in high positions were stealing millions of dollars at the expense of the taxpayers. Harding was once seen in the Red Room, standing with his hands around the throat of the Director of the Veterans Bureau, choking him and yelling, "You yellow rat! You double-crossing bastard!"

Let Us Entertain You

All Presidents have sought entertainment, and Thomas Jefferson was no exception. In 1771 he treated himself to three amusements: He paid three shillings to hear a concert of musical glasses, half that amount for an evening of "Dutch dancing and singing" and the same fee for seeing a live alligator. Also listed in his diary in 1786, he paid a shilling to watch a "learn'd pig" perform.

For Cryin' Out Loud

On August 31, 1901 Vice President Theodore Roosevelt attended Sunday services at the Dutch Reformed Church in Chicago. Following the sermon, the pastor invited Roosevelt to the pulpit to speak. Roosevelt made the most of this opportunity and spoke glowingly of the minister's sermon. The Vice President walked back and forth, speaking so loudly that a small child began to scream. Its screaming startled the 150 others in the congregation. The mother picked her child up and started to leave. Roosevelt said, "Sit down, please, madam. Don't go out. I have six of them of my own at home, and I am used to crying children." She returned to her seat, but the toddler continued screaming, forcing Roosevelt to shorten his talk. He left the pulpit and shook hands with each person present.

Fake Nose Blow

In February of 1898 President and Mrs. McKinley hosted a piano recital for twenty guests in the Blue Room. McKinley, however, was deeply distressed and needed to talk with someone. Noticing his friend and newspaperman H.H. Kohlsaat in attendance, the President motioned for him to come to the Red Room. Kohlsaat listened sympathetically as McKinley told of his wife's poor health. He had had almost no sleep the past two weeks. Congress and the public were demanding war with Spain. The Spanish fleet was in Cuban waters, and McKinley remarked that the U.S. didn't have "enough ammunition on the Atlantic seacoast to fire a salute." As he revealed his troubles, McKinley buried his face in his hands and began to sob. After calming himself he asked Kohlsaat, "Are my eyes very red? Do they look as if I have been crying?" Kohlsaat told him yes, knowing that the President must return to his guests. He suggested a plan: "When you open the door to enter the room, blow your nose very hard and loud. It will force tears into your eyes and they will think that is what made your eyes red." McKinley took the advice and, upon entering the Blue Room, gave a nasal blast heard by all.

Let's Move It!

The life of a professional soldier and his family can be adventurous, but often tedious. Mamie Eisenhower noted that she had moved 35 times in 35 years.

Pucker Parade

During the 1861 inaugural ceremonies, a float carrying 34 young girls passed the reviewing stand where Lincoln sat. Suddenly it stopped, and all 34 girls rushed over where each received a kiss from the new President.

Lost Generation

In describing hippies, the long-haired "flower children" of the 1960's and 1970's, Ronald Reagan said, " A hippie is someone who looks like Tarzan, walks like Jane, and smells like Cheetah."

Barred from Ballots

There is at least one voting ward in the U.S. where none of the residents can vote for any Presidential candidate. In Adams County, Wisconsin, all 500 residents are in a Federal Correctional Institution which covers the entire ward.

Strip and Stretch

In 1961 President Kennedy and his wife visited Paris. A palatial apartment at the Quai d'Orsay was set aside for the couple. Kennedy headed for the Chamber du Roi, the King's Chamber. The moment he entered the bedroom the exhausted President stripped to his birthday suit. He had reinjured his lower back at a tree planting ceremony in Ottawa a few weeks earlier, and the long ride home from the airport had been one of agony. An aide filled the bathtub and gave Kennedy an injection of Novocain. During his entire French visit he spent every available moment with hot water up to his chin. In fact, Kennedy spent much of his time in misery, having injured his back during World War II when his PT-109 was hit by a Japanese destroyer.

Editor's Deletion

In April of 1841 John Tyler hurriedly left his Williamsburg home, borrowed some money, and headed for Washington to assume the Presidency. After a month tenure Harrison was dead and Tyler took his oath. The country waited to see how Tyler would conduct affairs as he took over the reins of government. Would he be a mere figurehead, or a Chief Executive in his own right? After all, a President had never died in office. Tyler, however, left no

43

doubts to cabinet officials and congressmen. And when the first newspaper came to his desk, it was headlined "Acting President John Tyler." Calmly, the new President picked up a pen and crossed out the word "Acting."

Fast Learner

Millard Fillmore did not see a map of his country until he was nineteen years old. Up to that time, his exposure to books was confined to the Bible and a hymnal. Getting a late start on his schooling, the teenager fell in love with his teacher and later married her.

Bluntly Honest

John Quincy Adams was quite accurate in describing himself as "a man of reserve, cold, austere, and forbidding manner." While serving as President, he rose two hours before sunrise, walked four miles (in addition to "skinny dipping" in the Potomac during the summer), returned to make a fire, read three chapters in the Bible, then scanned the newspapers after breakfast. From 9 A.M. to 5 P.M., he received visitors, often without intermission. From 6 P.M. until midnight, he read official documents and government papers, then wrote in his diary.

Cold Turkey, er Canary

How cold is cold? At Grant's inaugural ball in 1873, guests found the celebration a bit chilly. They danced in an unheated pavilion just to keep warm. Canaries, which had been provided to serenade the guests, froze to death.

Boat Ride to D.C.

Several months after his 1960 defeat to John F. Kennedy, a somber Richard Nixon told the *New York Times*, "I was in the Navy in the South Pacific, but I wasn't on a P.T. boat. That's why I'm here and not in Washington."

Felled by a Question

In May of 1852 a well-known agnostic, Joseph Treat, arrived in Hiram, Ohio to lecture on the subject of religion and the Bible. Touring the country, Treat had already established himself as a great debater, much to the disappointment of many Christians. Treat won each debate and argument due to his sound logic and intellectual force. While addressing the audience in Hiram he denounced the organized church, the validity of the Scriptures, and the supposed corruption of religious leaders. Treat then invited the audience to ask questions regarding the Bible. Dramatically, a young classical scholar by the name of James Abram Garfield arose and posed the question,"What is the present participle of the verb 'to be'?" A dumbfounded Treat could not answer. At this point Garfield asked the audience how it could believe even one word by a man who claimed to be an expert on the Scriptures, but who did not know the simple rudiments of the language in which the New Testament was originally written. Such a demonstration not only delighted the audience, but firmly established Garfield as a man of faith, intellect and persuasion.

We Have Company

In 1863 the Lincolns entertained Mr. and Mrs. Tom Thumb, American's most famous dwarfs. During a White House dinner, Mary Lincoln ordered her son, Robert, to come downstairs and assist in entertaining the small couple. He must have felt it was below his dignity and he refused, telling his mother, "My notions of duty, perhaps, are somewhat different from yours."

Cincinnati Dodger

In 1840 William Henry Harrison did his best to avoid speaking on controversial issues. After all, he was running for President and did not want to offend anyone for fear of losing votes. A visitor from New York traveled to southwestern Ohio to find out Harrison's views on slavery and abolition. Harrison suggested, "There is no need of having any private conversation about politics. If you will stop and dine, I shall be happy to welcome you." Such evasive tactics worked, and Harrison unseated incumbent Martin Van Buren.

The Show's Over

Following Harding's sudden death, Calvin Coolidge was awakened and sworn in as the thirtieth President by his father, a minister and notary public. It was 2:47 A.M. on August 3, 1923, and Coolidge had shaved, dressed and waited for the oath. By the light of a kerosene lamp, in the presence of half a dozen witnesses, the son repeated the words of the father. Immediately following the ceremony, Coolidge turned to his guests and said, "Good night." He then went to bed.

Chief Inspector

Following his inauguration, James Monroe, set out on a journey to inspect the nation's coastal defenses and military posts. The trip lasted fourteen weeks and covered thirteen states. It was a triumphant success militarily and politically. Everywhere Monroe went he was greeted by large crowds, booming cannons and ringing church bells. He was a very popular President and his administration was dubbed as "The Era of Good Feeling."

Close Knit

Rutherford B. Hayes's relationship with his sister was not only close, but intense. He refused to attend her wedding and wrote her many passionate letters. Fanny was likewise in expressing her affection and wrote her brother that he was "daily the object of my waking thoughts and almost nightly of my dreams." When Fanny died after childbirth, Hayes told Lucy, his bride of four years, "You are sister Fanny to me now." The Hayeses had eight children, and their only daughter was named Fanny.

Hide and Seek

Though Calvin Coolidge was known for his silence and deadpan humor, he was also a prankster. On more than one occasion, the President would press all of the electric buttons on his desk and then hide underneath it. White House aides and secretaries rushed into the Oval Office only to find it empty. Coolidge always kept a straight face when relating this story.

A Fake Snake

Springtime comes early in Washington. In February of 1984 President Reagan was surprised to see snakes in the magnolia trees near the White House. It seems starlings had made a nuisance by staying there. The imitation snakes worked, and the birds stayed away.

Monumental Task

The Washington Monument was completed and dedicated on February 22, 1885, as President Chester Arthur presided over the ceremonies. It had taken nearly 38 years to construct!

Donation for a Donation

While attending Catholic church services one day, President Kennedy was sitting in a front pew where the offering plate was being passed. Kennedy had no money (as usual), so he asked his friend and Under Secretary of the Navy, Paul Fay, for a ten-dollar bill. Kennedy knew that all eyes would be watching him to see how much money he put in the offering. Fay had only a twenty-dollar bill which he quickly relinquished. The President proudly made his contribution while Fay was left penniless. The money was never paid back. With a twinkle in his eye, Kennedy remarked to Fay, "They should know they have a generous President."

Bad Actor

After Lincoln finished his inaugural address in 1865, he went inside the Capitol preparing to return to the White House. A young man broke through the police ranks and almost reached him. The police grabbed him and led him away. After questioning him, he was released after telling officers his name. It was John Wilkes Booth.

How About a Mule Ride?

While vacationing in California in 1957, Harry Truman refused to ride "Dumbo the Elephant" at Disneyland. The former President considered it a symbol of the Republican Party and did not want to be identified with it.

Wood-be Thieves

Two future Presidents, while visiting Shakespeare's birthplace in Stratford, England, cut chips off a wooden chair alleged to have been Shakespeare's and took them home as souvenirs. The two "culprits" were John Adams and Thomas Jefferson.

A Hair-Raising Experience

Going to and from school in Kentucky was quite an adventure for nine-year-old Zachary Taylor. One day in 1793 when several children were on their way home, they came to a fork in the forest path. The three Taylor brothers waved goodbye to their classmates and headed towards their log cabin. In an instant a piercing scream cut through the forest. A war party of Indians had split up to chase both groups of children. In the distance, the Taylors could hear their mother yelling for them to hurry. Arrows flew around them, and the boys fired their rifles at the band of warriors. Another shower of arrows followed and the boys zigzagged down the path to avoid being hit. In a final burst of speed, they reached the cabin as Mom slammed the door shut and placed a heavy wooden bar across it. The Indians tried to get in but failed. When all was safe, the boys learned that their schoolmates had been killed and scalped. Young Zach's experiences such as these led to a military career. He received a commission in the army from his distant cousin, Secretary of State James Madison. Taylor distinguished himself in four wars.

Two Future Presidents and The Stolen Apples

In November of 1840 President-Elect William Henry Harrison and his seven-year-old grandson Benjamin Harrison (the 23rd President) were walking through the streets of Cincinnati. During one long conversation between Grandpa and a friend, Little Ben walked over to an apple stand, filled his pockets, and took a bite of an extra apple. The woman in back of the stand said nothing until the two Harrisons began to leave. She screamed, "That boy did not pay me!" The President-Elect turned in surprise, walked over and placed a coin in her hand. Benjamin was not punished, because at their North Bend home anyone could have as many apples as they wanted — free. In fact, their orchards provided enough apples to hand out to the crowds during the 1840 election. Said Benjamin to his grandfather, "I didn't know apples ever cost money, Grandpa."

A Royal Rub

Theodore Roosevelt was appointed by President Taft in 1910 to represent the United States at the funeral of Kind Edward VII. Following the services, Germany's pompous Kaiser Wilhelm said to Roosevelt, "Call on me at two o'clock. I have just 45 minutes to give you." Roosevelt responded by saying, "I will be there at two, Your Majesty, but unfortunately I have but 20 minutes to give you."

When Was That?

Gerald Ford did not know the exact time he became President, but Henry Kissinger and Alexander Haig did. These two men were part of Nixon's White House staff. At precisely 11:35 a.m. on August 9, 1974, Secretary of State Kissinger initialed Nixon's statement of resignation, thus making it official. At noon, Gerald Ford was sworn in by Chief Justice Warren Burger, but technically Ford had already been President for 25 minutes.

Double Shift

Lyndon Johnson worked a two-shift day as President from 7:00 a.m. to 2:00 p.m., and from 4:00 to 9:00 p.m. His top assistants and aides, however, were "on call" at all times. Working under this arrangement, Johnson said, "It's like starting a new day."

The Eligibility List

President Martin Van Buren moved into the White House with his four bachelor sons. The President was also "available" since he had been a widower for nearly twenty years.

Tough and Rough

Historians tell us that George Washington, Andrew Jackson, U.S. Grant and Rutherford B. Hayes had many brushes with death on the battlefield. Perhaps overlooked are the close calls Theodore Roosevelt had while commanding his Rough Riders in Cuba during the Spanish-American War. On the third day after invading the island, T.R. was leaning against a tree when a bullet tore the bark away and filled his eyes with dust. Then a cannonball from a Spanish gun exploded near him, and he was hit with shrapnel. In his charge up Kettle Hill near San Juan, his horse got tangled in a wire fence. He dismounted as his men all around him fell. The colonel made no attempt to conceal himself from the enemy, and his orderly, while saluting him, fell mortally wounded across T.R.'s knees. Another soldier, with whom he was speaking, fell dead at his feet. Roosevelt's horse, "Little Texas," was scratched twice by bullets, one of which grazed the rider's elbow. Such daring and courage made Theodore a national hero.

I've Got My Own

The Whig Party nominated William Henry Harrison and John Tyler as its candidates in 1840. Harrison, as you know, was elected, but died after just one month in office. Tyler assumed the office and soon found himself "on the outs" with Whig leaders. Though rejected by political leaders, Tyler ran the government his own way. At a White House celebration, he invited 200 guests, prompting Tyler to remark, "They cannot now say I am a President without a party!"

A Town Appropriately Named

At the outbreak of the Civil War in 1861, Andrew Johnson was a U.S.

Senator. In a speech to his fellow legislators he had announced, "I love my country. I love the Constitution. Senators, my blood, my existence, I would give to save this Union." He nearly got to prove his point when he left the Capitol and headed for his home state of Tennessee to try to convince the citizens there to remain in the Union. On the train going south, Johnson stopped at a Virginia town where an angry mob dragged him by the coattails from the passenger car, spat upon him, fired pistols, threw punches at him, pulled his nose, fixed a noose around his neck, and tried to lynch him. But another senator from Texas intervened and convinced the crowd that Tennessee would like to hang its own traitor, and that they would solve nothing by hanging Johnson. Reason prevailed and the future President's life was spared. This incident, by the way, took place in *Lynch*burg, Virginia.

Busch Beer?

In September of 1988, George Bush visited the Pittsburgh Pirates' club-house. An avid fan and former collegiate player, Bush was happy to meet with the players while on the campaign trail. But left-handed pitcher Dave LaPoint must have gotten his Bushes mixed up. Remarked LaPoint, "I really like your beer!"

A Young Senior Citizen

Some Americans felt William Henry Harrison was too old to run for President in 1840. Having tried before and lost, the sixty-nine-year-old candidate became the overwhelming choice of the Whig Party to oppose the incumbent Martin Van Buren. Harrison must have regained his youth when, in October, a Whig rally was held by supporters in Madison County, Ohio. Presiding at this function was George Hempleman, age 108. One of the vice presidents was 99, another was 81 and a third was 79. All of the officers were veterans of the Revolutionary War.

Theories on Education

Our Chief Executives have had varying views on education. Thomas Jefferson once stated, "State a moral case to a plowman and a professor. The former will decide it as well, and often better than the latter, because he has not been led astray by artificial rules." James Madison felt that a government without public education "is but a prologue to a Farce or Tragedy, or perhaps both." John F. Kennedy recognized the worth of educators when he spoke of "modern cynics and skeptics who see no harm in paying those to whom we entrust the minds of our children a smaller wage than is paid to those they entrust the care of their plumbing." In 1965, Lyndon Johnson signed the Arts and Humanities Act into law and said, "Somehow the scientists always seem to get the penthouse while the arts and humanities get the basement." Ronald

Reagan, in referring to aid to education stated, "Why should we subsidize intellectual curiosity?"

Meet the Meatcutter

While living in Spencer County, Indiana, Abe Lincoln worked part time as a butcher. Working for farmers at the rate of 31¢ a day, Lincoln was seventeen years old at the time.

A Word to Remember

Prior to his December 8, 1941 speech before Congress, FDR substituted the word "infamy" after crossing out "history" as he asked for a declaration of war against Japan. The changing of this one word has made FDR's comment unforgettable.

They Made Me Do It

President William McKinley did not want war with Spain. But public pressure generated by "yellow journalism" and a vigorous pro-war effort by many congressmen demanded that America "flex her muscle." Spanish oppression of Cubans and insurrection in the Philippines provided a tempting opportunity for U.S. expansionists. After a brief and successful war, McKinley rode atop the popularity of military victories. But not all men of influence agreed with the administration's policies. According to professor-journalist William James, McKinley's philosophy was: "We are here for your own good, therefore unconditionally surrender to our tender mercies, or we'll blow you into kingdom come."

Jovial Giant

President Taft's White House bathtub could hold four men. It came from the *U.S.S. North Carolina*, a battleship whose commander had it specially installed when Taft stayed on the ship. The President weighed nearly 350 pounds, and comedians in the early 1900's joked that when Taft "went swimming in the Atlantic Ocean, nobody else could use it." The President was usually good-natured about his obesity, but one day during a parade in his honor, he was disturbed when many children greeted him with "Hello, Fatty."

A Diary Ditty

John Quincy Adams noted in his diary a rumor that Martin Van Buren was the illegitimate son of Aaron Burr. There is no conclusive evidence to support such an accusation.

James A. Garfield once observed, "The Sanctity of marriage and the family relation make the cornerstone of our American society and civilization."

Remember Me?

David Rice Atchison of Missouri was a U.S. President — for part of one day. As President pro-tem of the U. S. Senate, he became the legal head of the government between out-going Polk and in-coming Taylor on March 4, 1849. Ironically, Atchison was sleeping at the time he was the legal head of the government. On his tombstone is inscribed, "President of the U.S. one day." He died in 1886.

Bowling 'Em Over

Lincoln's favorite sport was bowling, but he was not very good at it. Though his scores were quite low, people crowded into the Washington gymnasium where he bowled because they enjoyed the young Congressman's jokes.

We Disagree

Susan B. Anthony visited the White House in March of 1884, bringing with her one hundred other delegates from a women's suffrage convention. She asked President Chester Arthur, "Ought not women to have full equality and political rights?" Said the 21st President, "We should probably differ on the details of that question."

Jealousy

Harry Truman, and many other men who had served in the U.S. Army, felt the Marines got too much publicity at the expense of the Army. The outspoken President regretted once saying that the "USMC had a more effective propaganda machine than Joseph Stalin."

A Burning Desire

Though elected President, James Monroe could not move into the White House for three years. It had been destroyed by the British and was not ready until the autumn of 1817.

Wrong Birthday

There have been numerous bloopers made by the media in covering news about our Presidents. One such newscaster made the following announcement: "And from Washington comes word that President and Mrs. Lincoln will spend Nixon's birthday at Key Biscayne, Florida on February 12th."

Look Me in the Eyes

In most of the photographs and illustrations portraying James Buchanan, his head is shown distinctly tilted. This led to a number of theories and accusations by critics as to the reason. Buchanan was nearsighted in one eye and farsighted in the other.

All Five

In 1945 when General Dwight Eisenhower was on his way back to Abilene, Kansas for a hero's reception, a reporter said to his mother, Ida, "You must be very proud of your son." She looked at the journalist, smiled and said, "Indeed I am. Which one are your talking about?" Ike's five brothers, Arthur, Edgar, Roy, Earl and Milton, were also very successful.

Safe Comment

When President and Mrs. Nixon visited China, a large banquet was held in their honor. When the First Lady was asked afterwards how she liked her meal, she responded by saying, "It was the best Chinese food I ever had."

Bosses Unsaddled

As support mounted for Teddy Roosevelt to become William McKinley's Vice President in 1900, Mark Hanna simply told him, "You're not fit for it." When T.R. became President after McKinley's death, political bosses and millionaire industrialists like Hanna soon discovered they had little control of the White House.

One That Backfired

Newspaper reporters were constantly frustrated that Calvin Coolidge said very little at press conferences, so they decided to play a little trick on the President. Forming a conspiracy prior to a press conference, every reporter wrote the exact same question on a piece of paper: "Are you going to run in 1928?" Coolidge read each slip in silence, making no expression. He then threw all the papers into the wastebasket. "Gentlemen," he said, "the only one of these questions I care to answer today is the one about public schools in Puerto Rico." Coolidge then delivered a long oration on that subject, citing facts and statistics. The journalists learned their lesson and never tried *that* trick again.

Being Prepared

President Theodore Roosevelt was a man of exceptional hardiness. At times, he would sneak away from the White House to go "skinny dipping" upriver in the Potomac. One time, his companion, the French Ambassador, forgot to remove his gloves before taking the plunge. "I think I will leave them on," he said, as he stood naked on the river bank. "We might meet some ladies."

Banner Years

In 1862 Andrew Johnson left his Greenville, Tennessee home to escape imprisonment by a confederate government. A banner was stretched across the main street proclaiming, "ANDREW JOHNSON, TRAITOR." Eight years later, having served a stormy term as post-Civil War President, he returned to Greenville to find another banner spanning the same spot. Only this one announced, "WELCOME HOME, ANDREW JOHNSON, PATRIOT."

He Never Knew

Actor Peter Graves and his wife were invited to a White House dinner by President and Betty Ford. Arriving from California to Dulles Airport in Washington, Graves telephoned the First Lady to explain they could not attend the dinner because the airline had lost their luggage. Betty Ford insisted they come anyway, telling Peter he could rent a suit and that his wife could choose one of the First Lady's dresses. While dancing that evening with Mrs. Graves, President Ford complimented her on the exquisite gown she was wearing, not realizing that it belonged to his wife.

Sobering Remark

It was during the 1858 Lincoln-Douglas debates for the U.S. Senate that Stephen Douglas reminded a crowd of his opponent's rather dismal career. He informed them that Lincoln had tried everything and had always been a failure. He had been a farmer and gave it up. He said Lincoln had tried flatboating and failed at that, had attempting teaching school and quit, had sold liquor in a saloon and failed at that, had tried preaching law with little success, and had gone into politics and was destined to follow the same course. When Douglas had finished his speech, Lincoln rose to reply. He came forward and said he was obliged to Douglas for the accurate history he had taken the trouble to compile. It was all true. Lincoln added, " I have worked the farm; I have split rails; I have worked on a flatboat; I have tried to practice law. There is just one thing Judge Douglas forgot to relate. He says I sold liquor over a counter. He forgot to tell you that, while I was on one side of the counter, the Judge was always on the other."

Take a Break

The observance of Christmas as a national holiday came late to the United States. In 1894, President Grover Cleveland was the first Chief Executive to give Christmas Day off to Civil Service workers.

I Have a Confession Not to Make

John F. Kennedy fulfilled his obligation to attend confession and tried to make arrangements so the priest never knew whose confession he was hearing. However, this was not always possible. One time, when Kennedy entered the confessional booth, he was greeted with the words, "Good evening, Mr. President." Responded JFK, "Good evening, Father," and he quickly exited.

A Case of Slander

In 1915, the *Washington Post* made a monumental "boo-boo" when it printed an article describing President Woodrow Wilson's courtships of Edith Galt, a widow. "The President spent much of the evening *entering* Mrs. Galt ..." The story should have used the word "entertaining," and the editors at the *Post* tried desperately to retrieve the paper from the newsstands, but copies had already been sold. Wilson's first wife had been dead for only a year and a half, before he and Mrs. Galt were married in a Presbyterian church.

A Breath of Fresh Air

Richard Nixon did not think too highly of the media. On Presidential trips, some of the press got to travel on *Air Force One* with the President. On one such occasion, Nixon left the reporters and went to the back of the plane. Commenting to some stewards and Secret Service agents, Nixon quipped, "It sure smells better back here, doesn't it?" Word of this remark leaked out, further damaging the President's relationship with the press.

Rot Gut

President Garfield did not like Chief Sitting Bull. Neither did he like the White House meals that were served to him as he lay dying from infection caused by an assassin's bullet. Confined to a strict bland diet, the President was informed that the great Sioux warrior was starving. Garfield exclaimed, "Let him starve." Then he corrected himself and voiced a crueler fate: "Oh no, send him my oatmeal."

Humbly Honored

Ronald Reagan was great with "one-liners." When the President visited his alma mater at Eureka College in Illinois, he was presented an honorary doctorate degree. A humbled President remarked to those attending that the ceremony was "a happening which only compounded an already heavy burden of guilt. I had always figured the *first* degree you gave me was honorary."

Never Say Never

While stationed in California with the Army in 1853, U.S. Grant joined the Sons of Temperance and took an oath never to drink alcoholic beverages. But loneliness, poverty and gloom gave way to whiskey. On two occasions, he came dangerously close to being court-martialed for drunken behavior, and in April of the following year, he resigned from the Army and returned east to his family. Hard times and more drinking would follow, but the Civil War gave Grant an opportunity to demonstrate his talents of military command.

After<u>math</u>

After Lincoln was voted out of Congress, he felt the need to further his education. Studying geometry, he took several months to read the six volumes of Euclid.

Now Listen, Doctor

In 1833 Andrew Jackson was a sick man, suffering from internal bleeding. After an examination by a physician, the President promptly informed the doctor, "There are only two things I can't give up; one is coffee, and the other is tobacco."

Bring on the Food

The Grants entertained lavishly at the White House. At times the First Family served thirty-course dinners, including exotic dishes of nightingale tongues and leg of partridge. It was not wonder the President gained fifty pounds in one year.

Devoted Fans

Many of our Chief Executives have had a fondness for baseball. Consider Herbert Hoover's comment: "I shall tell my doctors baseball has more curative powers than all their medicine." And Dwight Eisenhower once remarked, "The more baseball the better. It is a healthful sport and develops team play and initiative, plus an independent attitude."

Say It Ain't So!

George Washington flew into rages over the gazettes (newspapers) criticizing his administration. The first President constantly complained that the numerous daily publications made it impossible for him to govern. Sounds familiar, doesn't it?

Kiss From a Miss That Missed

On graduation day in 1901, Harry Truman's English teacher, Miss Tillie, kissed Charley Ross, the best scholar in her class (Truman was the second best). When asked why she had done this only to Ross, Miss Tillie smiled and explained, " I hope yet to kiss a President of the United States." Ross later became Press Secretary to President Harry Truman.

And the Band Played On

Marine Band concerts are held regularly on the White House lawns during spring and summer seasons. This tradition was begun by the Tyler administration.

A Sour Note

When Lincoln was shot, his brown leather wallet was removed and the contents examined. In it were several newspaper clippings and another surprising item — a five-dollar Confederate note!

Bedtime Story

In June of 1982 President Reagan visited Pope John Paul II in the Vatican. The event was televised live as the Pope delivered a discourse on the futility of war. With millions of views watching, Ronald Reagan fell asleep.

No Rest

After retiring from the White House James and Dolley Madison thought they might enjoy some relaxation and privacy. How wrong they were. During the first few summers, throngs of guests and curiosity-seekers visited them at their Virginia estate, Montpelier. Outside, under shade trees, the Madisons spread dinner for as many as ninety guests at a time.

George's Roots

George Washington's ancestry has been traced to the early 1200's in England. One of his forefathers, William Weshington, is recorded on the roll of royal knights.

Sign Here My Children

With promises of money, whiskey, annual gifts and hunting grounds, William Henry Harrison obtained more than 60,000,000 acres of land for the United States. As military leader of western territories in the early 1800's, Harrison persuaded scores of Indian chiefs to cede land to the "17 Fires" (The U.S.) and the "Great Father" (Thomas Jefferson). Harrison promised the tribes (he referred to them as his "children") eternal peace but often ignored Indian pleas for justice and fair play. Squatters and thousands of settlers moved in on Indian lands as the government refused to enforce the treaties. Jefferson praised Harrison's land-grabbing practices, but Indian leaders like Tecumseh, Blue Jacket, Shabbona and Red Eagle claimed the agreements were immoral and illegal. The amount of land the government received via treaties equaled an area larger than the entire state of Wisconsin. But bloodshed continued for decades to come.

Editor's Error

Dwight Eisenhower and his brother, Edgar, both graduated from high school in 1909 in Abilene, Kansas. The senior yearbook predicted that Edgar would serve two terms as President of the United States, and that Dwight would be a professor at Yale.

Absence of Adolescence

Noted educator and historian Edward Everett Hale felt that John Quincy Adams was an exceptional child, and observed, "There seemed to be in his life no such stage as boyhood."

Living Words

The Civil War had not been going well for the Union. Rumors within the government, including President Lincoln's cabinet, persisted that the "Rail-splitter" from Illinois should be and would be replaced. When Secretary of the

Treasury Salmon P. Chase learned that Lincoln was going to Gettysburg to make a speech and dedicate the battlefield, he referred to the President's trip as "the dead going to eulogize the dead."

Girl Crazy

Many bachelors tried to win the hand of Alice Roosevelt, the beautiful and spirited daughter of our 26th President. Barons, dukes and millionaires alike from America and abroad contended for courting her. One day at the Roosevelt mansion at Sagamore Hill, New York, a stranger drove up in a buggy and told the guard at the gate that he had an appointment with the President. This same caller told the Secret Service man that he was going to marry Alice. The intruder was ordered away but whipped his horse toward the house. A scuffle ensued as a couple of guards wrestled the man to the ground. A revolver was found on the floorboards of the buggy, and the man was jailed. Police officers informed the President that they felt the suspect was a deranged publicity-seeker. Papa Theodore commented, "Of course he's insane. He wants to marry Alice!"

Oh, What A Feelin'!

John Adams's feelings for the feminine gender began stirring when he was just ten years old. According to his own account, he spent many evenings in the company of "modest and virtuous girls," remarking also that "no Virgin or Matron ever had cause to blush at the sight of me or to regret her Acquaintance with me."

You Better Listen

While seeking reelection as Governor of Tennessee in 1855, Andrew Johnson gave speeches with his papers in one hand and a revolver in the other. It was a turbulent time throughout the country, and Johnson made many enemies with his pro-Union stance. He was reelected, and two years later was elected to the U.S. Senate.

Bumming a Ride

On a western train trip in 1919, Woodrow Wilson's Secret Service agents discovered two hoboes trying to hitch a ride under one of the President's railroad cars. When the bums found out whose train it was, they asked an agent, "Do you think he would shake hands with fellows like us?" Both the President and the First Lady stepped forward and shook their hands, and even offered them a ride. The hoboes declined.

Cursed Memento

Under pressure to resign, even though there was no Vice President, Richard Nixon was urged by advisors to send Gerald Ford's name to Congress for confirmation. In late 1973 Nixon signed the document making Ford his Vice President. Nixon sent his advisor, Fred Buzhardt, a souvenir and commented, "Here's the damn pen I signed Jerry Ford's nomination with."

That's All, Folks

How does a President cut short an interview while boarding his helicopter? He, or his press secretary, simply makes a signal to the pilot to rev up the engines, creating a swirl of air and drowning out any human voices!

Embarrassing

Once, while Lincoln was practicing law in Springfield, Illinois, he tore the seat of his pants just before his appearance in court. The other attorneys circulated a paper to ask donations for a new pair of pants. When the paper came to him, instead of signing his name for a contribution, Lincoln wrote, " I can contribute nothing to the end in sight."

Winning At Any Cost

In a game of checkers with Under Secretary of the Navy, Paul Fay, John Kennedy was getting beaten. Kennedy had challenged Fay to a game of chess but deferred to checkers, only to discover Fay was about to win the game. Kennedy suddenly coughed, then sent the checkerboard and pieces flying off the table. Remarked the President, "One of those unfortunate incidents in life, Redhead. We'll never know if the Under Secretary was going to strategically outmaneuver the Commander-in-Chief." They played two other games, and Kennedy won them both. Such was JFK's obsession to win.

Self-Proclaimed Hero of "Fire Water"

In the autumn of 1812, a band of Wyandots and Shawnees led by Tecumseh attacked Fort Harrison in the Indiana Territory. The small garrison was manned by fifty American soldiers, led by a future President. During the attack several barrels of whiskey inside the fort exploded, creating a huge fire and infuriating the commander. The young captain in charge, later describing the event, spared no praise for himself. He commented he had "remained firmly in command" and that "my presence of mind did not for a moment forsake me." He further hinted that his genius and bravery under fire merited a promotion. In spite of his self-proclaimed greatness, the captain had to wait for nearly two weeks before 1200 soldiers rescued him from 300 Indians. Promotion for this officer inside Fort Harrison would come 35 years later when he won victories against the Mexicans. And not long after that, he was elected as our 12th President — Zachary Taylor.

You Make Me Sick!

In the 1940 film "Knute Rockne — All American," Ronald Reagan co-starred with Pat O'Brien. O'Brien played Rockne, and Reagan played the part of the legendary Notre Dame running back, George Gipp. During the making of the film, Reagan had to run an 80-yard touchdown. The scene had to be shot three times. The third take was too much for the young actor, and he vomited his bacon and egg sandwich he had eaten for lunch.

Personal Questions

CBS's Morley Safer asked First Lady Betty Ford how she would respond if her daughter came to her and said she was having an affair. Mrs. Ford began her answer by saying, "Well, I wouldn't be surprised; I think she's a perfectly normal human being like all young girls." This provoked an outcry across the country. And when Jimmy Carter was asked the same question, he stated that he would "be shocked and overwhelmed. But then my daughter is only seven."

I Can't Do It

One of Benjamin Harrison's campaigners, Matthew Quay of Pennsylvania, wasn't certain he wanted to work for Harrison's election in 1888. He was reluctant, referring to Harrison as the "White House Iceberg." Quay was the G.O.P. Chairman in 1888.

Rutherford B. Hayes was a champion speller in school. Proving himself by winning almost every spelling bee, he boasted, "Not one in a thousand could spell me down."

Cleared At Last

In 1979, Jimmy Carter exonerated Dr. Samuel Mudd for his alleged involvement in the Lincoln conspiracy. Dr. Mudd had set John Wilkes Booth's broken leg on the night of Lincoln's assassination, and was found guilty of plotting with Booth. Sentenced to hard labor for life at Devil's Island, Mudd was later released for ending a typhoid epidemic there. But it was not until 110 years later that his name and honor were restored.

Beast Feast

Thinking about his upcoming trip to Africa, Theodore Roosevelt once told a friend in the House of Representatives, "Congressmen, I wish I had those sixteen lions to turn loose on Congress." The Congressman asked T.R. if he didn't think that the lions might make a mistake and eat the wrong members of Congress. Roosevelt flashed his toothy smile and replied, "They would not make any mistakes if they stayed long enough."

Seams Important

Millard Fillmore, like Andrew Johnson, was a tailor. In 1820, Fillmore worked in Erie County, New York, at his father's shop. A local judge took an interest in Fillmore and financed his education through law school.

Late at the Plate

George Washington was always prompt, and he expected the same of others. Once a Congressman arrived a little late to a dinner in the Executive Mansion, only to discover the other guests were already eating. Washington told him, "We are obliged to be punctual here. My cook never asks whether the company has arrived, but whether the hour has."

No Grunt From Grant

Grant spoke very few words prior to his death. For several weeks before succumbing to throat cancer in 1885, he could not speak. His questions and responses were written on paper.

Jefferson said of Andrew Jackson's quest for President, "He is one of the most unfit men I know for such a place. He has very little respect for laws or constitutions."

Left Left Out

Ronald Reagan made no apologies for being conservative, or "far right" politically. At a gridiron dinner in 1981, he told an audience of broadcasters and reporters about his new administration, "Sometimes the right hand doesn't know what the far right hand is doing."

Managing the Money

Lincoln was not a good administrator and understood finances very little. He left financing the Civil War to his Secretary of Treasury, Salmon P. Chase. The war was costing the government a staggering sum of $2,500,000 each day, but Lincoln had no grasp of the problem. He went so far as to say he "had no money sense."

Just Ask Me

During the campaign of 1960, Democratic candidate John Kennedy criticized his opponent, Vice President Richard Nixon, for not really being much of a leader in formulating policy. This found some truth when reporters asked President Eisenhower what major decisions Nixon had participated in during his eight years as the number two man. Said Eisenhower, "If you give me a week, I might think of one." Kennedy won the election by a very slim margin.

Due Credit

Teddy Roosevelt and Woodrow Wilson are the Presidents given the most credit for creating the Panama Canal. Yet it was William Howard Taft as Secretary of War, and later as Chief Executive, who handled the enormous difficulties of seeing the project through. Conquering disease, figuring out logistics, and providing finances and manpower all fell on Taft's shoulders. Taft also was instrumental in working out a solution to end the Japanese-Russo War when he served as mediator, but Roosevelt was awarded the Nobel Peace Prize. Needless to say, historians have overlooked the contribution of the gentleman from Cincinnati.

William McKinley knew nothing about football, nor did he enjoy watching it. Once, when he and his friend Mark Hanna attended a game, the 25th President kept asking Hanna what was going on. Ironically, McKinley is buried across the road from the Professional Football Hall of Fame in Canton, Ohio.

Achtung!

During World War II, President Roosevelt's patience with critical reporters sometimes ran out. FDR once told a reporter to go stand in a corner. On another occasion, the 32nd President presented a newspaper man with a German Iron Cross because of his critical remarks during World War II.

Climbing to the Top

It was March 1864. Following U.S. Grant's commission and Lincoln's White House reception in the General's honor, Grant was ushered out of the reception before he was mobbed by an over-enthusiastic crowd. He and his son, Frederick, hurried to a hotel. The desk clerk looked at the poorly dressed, bearded soldier and stated, "The only room I have is a little one up in the attic." Grant humbly replied, "That will do." After signing his name in the hotel register, the surprised clerk gasped, "Are *you* Ulysses S. Grant?" Oh excuse me, sir. Yes, yes, General Grant, I have an elegant room for you." "No. Just put us in the little one," the General stated. Father and son then went up to their hot, cramped and dusty quarters. The next day, Grant officially became General of the Armies and no man but George Washington had ever before held that title.

No Fear

Less than a year before James A. Garfield was gunned down by a disappointed office-seeker, he told Senator John Sherman, "Assassination can no more be guarded against than death by lightning; and it is best not to worry about either."

Who Are They?

As far back as 1888, Viscount Bryce, an English historian answered the question, "Why Great Men Are Not Chosen Presidents." "Three reasons for this are 1) because great men are rare in politics; 2) because the method of choice does not bring them to the top; and 3) because they are not, in quiet times, absolutely needed." And author James Michener has written, "One has to come to grips with why we pass up great men to be President. We pass them up because we don't want first class men in that position; we want somebody who is a stupid bum like us. We really are in quite serious trouble."

Joseph Kennedy's Bankroll

The Kennedys of Massachusetts spent a lot of money in getting John elected President. Opponents charge that Papa Kennedy invested millions of dollars to get his son into the White House. The candidate joked about the charges that he was trying to buy the West Virginia primary. "I got a wire from my father: 'Dear Jack. Don't buy one more vote than necessary. I'll be damned if I'll pay for a landslide.' "

Free At Last

It was a slave owner who helped free slaves. U. S. Grant obtained several slaves upon his marriage to Julia Dent of Missouri. Prior to the Civil War they were given their freedom.

Un-comforting Words

Many Presidents have had a propensity for small talk, while others simply could not communicate very well. Richard Nixon not only found it difficult to chat with individuals but his stiff formality and inability to relax usually led him to say the wrong thing at the wrong time. On Veterans Day in 1969, he visited a Washington D.C. hospital and told a one-eyed Vietnam veteran, "All you need is one. You see too much anyway."

On Target

Artillery officer Harry Truman led his unit through World War I with just two casualties— one killed and one wounded. Having replaced two other commanders who could not control the men, Truman's strict but fair leadership earned him honors and respect.

A Third Opinion

When John Quincy Adams was eight years old, he fractured his right forefinger in a fall. Two doctors urged that it be amputated in order to save his entire hand. But the boy's mother, Abigail, hired a third physician who saved the finger. The doctor was Joseph Warren, hero of the Revolutionary War, who was killed at the Battle of Bunker Hill.

What A Relief!

Thomas Jefferson claimed he got headaches, often severe, every day for eight years while he was President. The day after leaving office his headaches were no more.

Not So Funny

Lee and Grant met just one time after the Civil War. On May 1, 1869 Lee received an invitation to the White House. A president of Washington University (now Washington and Lee), the famous general was seeking funds to build a railroad into Lexington, Virginia near his college. The two men met and shook hands. Lee mentioned to Grant why he was in the city, and Grant replied in jest, "You and I, General, have had more to do with destroying railroads than building them." Lee did not find the remark very amusing, but stayed twenty more minutes to talk to President Grant.

A Lion's Share

Teddy Roosevelt had many powerful enemies, particularly among financiers and industrialists who were targets of T.R.'s effort to break up monopolies and big trusts. When Roosevelt left the country on a well-publicized African safari, a large painted sign appeared at the New York Stock Exchange: "Wall Street Expects Every Lion To Do Its Duty."

Dog's Best Friend

Said Lyndon Johnson, "The fact that dogs haven't given up on humans completely and still make people their friends shows there must be some hope for the human race."

I'm First, By George!

Legally, the first U.S. President was John Adams. He took his oath of office as Vice President nine days before George Washington was sworn in. George was out of town and, according to the Constitution, was unable to act as President, therefore yielding those powers to the Vice President.

Solitary Man

As a boy growing up in Whittier, California, Richard Nixon occasionally climbed up into a bell tower of an old church his father had converted into a grocery store, and sat there for hours on end reading and thinking. Nixon's passion for privacy and solitude was a habit which kept him isolated from the public and the media as President.

"Locked" Into Place

Until the locomotive came along, Ohio had the most impressive network of canals in the country. Drawn by mules or horses, vessels of various shapes and sizes transported people and cargo along 300 miles of the "big ditch." Not everyone, however, was impressed. In 1843, John Quincy Adams boarded a packet (passenger boat) in Ohio and described his journey: "So much humanity crowded into such a compass was a trial such as I had never before experienced, and I reflected that I am to pass three nights and four days in it. The most uncomfortable part of our navigation is caused by the careless and unskillful steering of the boat in and through the locks, which seem to be numberless. The boat scarcely escapes a heavy thump on entering every one of them. She strikes and grazes against their sides and staggers along like a stumbling nag."

Spank that Yank

Lincoln was constantly criticized by high-ranking officers for interfering with the harsh disciplining of Union soldiers. The President pardoned many a Yankee who had been designated for the firing squad. A fourteen-year old boy was once court-martialed and sentenced to death. Upon hearing the news, Lincoln issued a pardon recommending, "spanking instead of shooting."

Whiskers for Gracy

Lincoln's beard came about due to the request of an eleven-year-old, Grace Bedell of Westfield, New York. In a letter dated October 15, 1860, the young lady wrote the Presidential candidate, "I have four brothers and part of them will vote for you anyway and if you will let your whiskers grow I will try to get the rest of them to vote for you. You would look a great deal better for your face is thin. All the ladies like whiskers and they would tease their husbands to vote for you and then you would be President." Later, when the Lincoln train stopped in Westfield, the President-elect sought out Grace in a crowd, picked her up, and presented her with a kiss.

Not Stripped of Rank

During World War II, FDR made Sherry Britton an honorary Brigadier General. At the time, she was the most popular stripper and pin-up girl in the country.

A Stitch in Time

While being interviewed by *Playboy* magazine in 1976, Jimmy Carter took out a needle and thread to repair a tear in his jacket. "Say, do you always do your own sewing?" asked the interviewer. As Carter bit off the thread with his teeth, he responded, "Uh-huh."

Head of the House

At the age of just fourteen, Tom Jefferson became head of his family when his father died in 1757. There was his mother and seven other children to care for, but Peter Jefferson had left his family a sizable fortune. Perhaps this burden of responsibility and management prepared young Thomas for leading a nation.

Food Facts

Ulysses S. Grant could not stand the sight of blood. Even though he lost thousands of men during the Civil War, the famed general got sick at the dinner table if his meat was too red. Grant also breakfasted on sliced cucumbers and vinegar sauce. John F. Kennedy was known to have eaten huge quantities of clam chowder at one sitting. James Buchanan devoured large portions of sauerkraut mixed with mashed potatoes. Tom Jefferson soaked much of his food in olive oil. But Gerald Ford's fetish outranks them all. For breakfast he often enjoyed cottage cheese drowned in ketchup!

Designated Hitter?

In 1910 people throughout North America had a right to be concerned. Halley's Comet came so close to earth that millions feared a catastrophe. Its light was simply brilliant, and its length in the heavens equaled the amount of 22 moons. Though fear and superstition gripped the country, political cartoonist saw the situation in a different light. U.S. newspapers pictured Teddy Roosevelt with a baseball bat knocking the comet away, with a caption stating, "The comet found out that Teddy was on earth."

Don't Trust An Abstainer

Sam Houston's description of James K. Polk was somewhat less than complimentary when he referred to the eleventh President as "a victim of the use of water as a beverage." Polk, a non-drinker, also differed greatly with Sam Houston on the principles of secession and slavery.

Lullaby

At a White House dinner in 1910 President Taft entertained his cabinet members and their wives. Following the meal, Taft insisted on some music from the record player but fell asleep before the song was finished. He woke up and requested another song but dozed off before it was completed. While Taft snored, his attorney general selected a rousing tune and played it loudly. The president continued to slumber, and led the attorney general to exclaim, "He must be dead!"

Little Things in Big Packages

In early 1865 Grant and Lincoln were on board ship to meet with representatives of the Confederacy to discuss peace terms. Representing the rebel states was Alexander Stephens, who had known Lincoln years before in Congress. Stephens was a very small man, weighing only 90 pounds. Lincoln moved toward the little Georgian and noticed he was wearing a huge overcoat. The Confederate Vice President removed his large overcoat, unwrapped several shawls and a long woolen muffler. The smiling Lincoln offered a handshake, then remarked to Stephens, "Never have I seen so small a nubbin come out of so much husk." Grant told of this incident many times.

Nixon Nixed

Harry Truman once said that Richard Nixon was "a no-good lying bastard. He can lie out of both sides of his mouth at the same time, and if he ever caught himself telling the truth he'd lie to keep his hand in." Jimmy Carter must have agreed, and in 1974 stated, "In two hundred years of history, he's the most dishonest President we've ever had."

To The Victor Belongs the Spoils

Theodore Roosevelt's teenage daughter, Alice, was well-known for her shocking comments and behavior. One of her remarks concerned the less-than-delicious White House meals: "Anyone who got anything good to eat there brought it in a paper bag."

"Phamus Fourfather"

George Washington would not have fared too well in a spelling bee. Even as an adult, his command of English was less than satisfactory. His diary provides us with some amusing variations of words. Here is a small sample of his spelling: road (rode), kalendar (calendar), liquods (liquids), shew (show), recied (received), etarnall (eternal), catched (caught), baricoota (barracuda), and Fryday (Friday).

71

Grassroots Philosophy

John F. Kennedy promoted volunteerism on a large scale. Kennedy once said, "Every time we try to lift a problem from our own shoulders and shift it to the government, to the same extent we are sacrificing the liberties of our people." Later Presidents, namely Reagan and Bush, also advocated solving many of our problems with local volunteer efforts.

Alias

John Adams was also known as "Novanglus." This was the pseudonym he used when he wrote a series of articles for the *Boston Gazette* prior to the Revolutionary War.

That's My Boy

Harry Truman's mother once explained, "... I've known that boy would amount to something from the time he was nine years old. He never did anything by halves." Even in his teens, Truman gained a reputation for responsibility and hard work. A railroad construction foreman recommended him highly for future employment by remarking, "Harry's all right. He's all right from his navel out in every direction."

Playing the Right Hand

During the Civil War the U.S. and England came dangerously close to war. Great Britain needed the South's cotton, and several incidents on the high seas brought disfavor upon Union shipping policy. Lincoln was besieged by visitors and reporters asking if he would declare war on England. The President grew tired of such requests and answered one inquiry with the following parable: "Your question reminds me of an incident which occurred out west. Two roughs were playing cards for high stakes, when one of them, suspecting his adversary of foul play, straightaway drew his bowie-knife from his belt and pinned the hand of the other player upon the table, exclaiming, 'If you haven't got the ace of spades under your palm, I'll apologize.' "

Celebrity Status

Two Presidents are buried in a Hollywood cemetery! James Monroe and John Tyler were laid to rest there. Incidentally, Hollywood Cemetery is located in *Richmond, Virginia.*

Up, Up and Away

LBJ loved extravagance and ordered that *Air Force One* be outfitted with an exercise bicycle. While flying 600 miles per hour, the President pumped away on his machine clad in a sweat suit.

He Couldn't Even Say Thanks

In 1759 a new young delegate was introduced into Virginia's House of Burgesses — his name was George Washington. Having returned from the French and Indian War as a hero, the assembly met to officially thank him for his services to the colonies. Washington rose to reply, but could make none. The nervous delegate blushed, stammered, and trembled, unable to utter a word. The House Speaker then addressed the young officer, "Sit down, Mr. Washington. Your modesty equals your valor, and that surpasses the power of any language I possess."

Getting Off The Hook

While attending a large rally in Kentucky during his campaign for the Presidency in 1960, John F. Kennedy was asked by a proud Kentuckian if the most beautiful women came from Kentucky, or from Massachusetts (JFK's home state). Ever the quick wit, Kennedy explained that, since his wife was from New York, the most beautiful women came from *that* state.

I Remember Mama

The first woman James Garfield kissed after being sworn in was not his wife. He kissed his mother, the only President to do so on this occasion.

Pox From the Chief

Constantly besieged by office seekers each week, Lincoln could only find rest from the hordes when he was sick. Following his Gettysburg Address, the President contracted smallpox. He yelled to a friend, "I now have something I can give to everybody." Newspapers told stories of job hunters suddenly fleeing the White House upon hearing what ailed the President.

The Fall Guy

Senator Albert Fall of New Mexico became the only cabinet member in history to go to jail. This was during the Harding administration while Fall served as Secretary of the Interior. But even before the Teapot Dome scandals, Fall's dishonesty and conniving preceded him. Bitterly opposed to President Wilson's plan for the U.S. to enter the League of Nations, Fall was also convinced that Wilson was either dead or completely incapacitated after his stroke in 1919. He demanded to see the President, and the First Lady and Doctor Grayson granted his request. Called to the White House to see for himself, Fall met the bed-stricken Wilson. Upon entering the bedroom, Fall was told by the President, "I hope the Senator will now be reassured, but he may be disappointed." After their conversation, Fall bent over the Chief Executive and took his right hand. "Mr. President," he said, "I am praying for you." Wilson looked up at him and sheepishly replied, "Which way, Senator?"

"Phoney" Concern?

A President's time is valuable. A Nixon staff member once recommended to the President that he telephone a Republican senator who was dying. But Chief of Staff Bob Haldeman argued that Nixon should not have to make two phone calls, when just one could be made to the widow in a few days. Thus, the suggestion was turned down with the command, "Wait until he dies."

A Toast or a Roast?

John Quincy Adams was very independent, stubborn and determined. Both Republicans and Federalists disliked him. While Adams was President, a toast was made in his behalf. Reportedly a colleague raised a glass and said, "May he always strike confusion to his foes!" Daniel Webster, sitting nearby, remarked, "As he has already done to his friends."

Bottled Up in the White House

James Buchanan once chastised his liquor merchants for sending small bottles of champagne to the Executive Mansion, explaining "Pint bottles are very inconvenient in this house, as the article is not used in such small quantities."

Prophets' Profits

Thomas Jefferson and Alexander Hamilton differed greatly on their concept of government. Hamilton, a Federalist, opposed Jefferson on many points of view. Yet the third President liked Hamilton and found him honest and sincere. Regarding Hamilton's ideas, Jefferson said, "In a contest between profit and patriotism, patriotism is likely to come off second best. He who stands to make the profit will not lack for arguments to convince himself that to do so is in the country's best interest."

A Mixed Bag?

It has been charged that Warren Harding's background was of mixed racial blood — Negro and Caucasian. The 29th President once admitted to a friend, "How do I know? One of my ancestors may have jumped the fence."

74

A "Heavy" Price Tag

Nancy Reagan's 1985 inaugural gown cost $25,000. But Ida McKinley's dress in 1901 may have been just as expensive at today's prices. Made of expensive red satin, it was adorned with many pearls, and was so heavy that the frail Mrs. McKinley toppled over during the ball.

Who's Who

According to Lincoln's law partner, William Herndon, the future President once inquired, "Did you ever notice that bastards are generally smarter, shrewder, and more intellectual that others? Is it because (these characteristics are) stolen?" Rumors surfaced on more that one occasion that Lincoln's parentage was suspect. Just *maybe* he could readily identify with this predicament. Research by some biographers years after Lincoln's death declared both Lincoln and his mother were of illegitimate birth, but the evidence, though inconclusive, can be considered strongly circumstantial.

Is It Possible?

George Washington *did* live in the White House! For three months after his marriage to Martha Custis, the Washingtons lived at Martha's estate which was officially called "White House." While residing there, George took his seat in the House of Burgesses at Williamsburg.

Faint Praise

Whether well-known American writer William Cullen Bryant regretted the death of President William Henry Harrison in 1841, one cannot say. But Bryant did say it was a shame Harrison just lived one month "only because he did not live long enough to prove his incapacity for the office of President."

Speaking in "General Terms"

Lincoln was constantly prodding General George B. McClellan to take the offensive against Robert E. Lee. The general, nicknamed "Little Napoleon," was an egocentric visionary who was often insubordinate and highly critical of the President. He even implied that Lincoln was a traitor and complained he never had enough men and supplies when, in fact, his forces greatly outnumbered the enemy. On two occasions, McClellan publicly snubbed the President, but the patient Lincoln remarked, "I will hold McClellan's horse if he will only bring us success." After hearing Lincoln say, "McClellan has the slows," the general wrote a sarcastic note to his Commander-in-Chief, "Have captured two cows. What disposition should I make of them?" Replied the President, "Milk 'em, George." Given every opportunity to fulfill his promise of victory,

McClellan was eventually replaced, only to run against Lincoln for the Presidency in 1864.

Mamie's Namesake

Eisenhower's first *Air Force One* plane was a Lockheed Constellation (he used three of them while in office). He named each of them "Columbine" after the blue Colorado flower of his wife's home state.

Motherly Advice

William McKinley's mother once told a friend, "No boy will ever be President who is afraid of hard work . . . I think religion is a great benefit to a boy."

Mechanical Midget

Richard Nixon possessed little knowledge of mechanical devices. His top aide, Bob Haldeman, admitted that Nixon "was the least dexterous man I have ever known; clumsy would be too elegant a word to describe his mechanical aptitude." Finding a tape recorder that the President could operate was a "major project" and no matter how many times he flew on *Air Force One*, Nixon never mastered the simple controls that adjusted his Presidential chair. He couldn't even figure out how to operate the various spotlights over his desk and chair, and the stereo system in his compartment was a complete mystery to him.

Patriotism

Teddy Roosevelt had a definition for those people living in the United States. He said, "Any man who says he is an American but something else also, isn't an American at all. We have room for but one flag, the American flag."

Big Spender

In 1932 President Herbert Hoover asked a colleague for a nickel to buy a friend a soda. The President was told, "Here's a dime. Treat them all!"

"Mum" is the Word

In 1922 Governor Channing Cox of Massachusetts visited his predecessor Calvin Coolidge, then Vice President of the U.S. Cox asked Coolidge how he had been able to see so many visitors each day and still leave the governor's office at 5:00 p.m., whereas Cox himself usually left several hours later. Cox inquired of the Vice President, "Why the difference?" Coolidge replied, "You talk back."

Somebody Name Me!

For six weeks U.S. Grant had no name. Finally the family convened to put their choices on slips of paper, and Grandma's selection of Ulysses (after the ancient Greek hero) was picked. Grandpa, however, was quite upset because his suggestion was not chosen. There was compromise, and the name Hiram Ulysses was given to the baby. But all through his adolescent years, friends and family called the boy Sam.

Comments of Condemnation

Not all blacks were impressed by Abraham Lincoln. Harvard graduate and activist W.E.B. DuBois described the 16th President as "a southern poor white, of illegitimate birth, poorly educated and unusually ugly, awkward, ill-dressed. He liked smutty stories and was a politician down to his toes . . . he was big enough to be inconsistent — cruel, merciful, peace-loving, a fighter . . ." Another well-known author, Edgar Lee Masters (from Illinois), said Lincoln's record in Congress was "a tracing of his wavering mind, his incoherent thinking . . . he was an undersexed man."

Choice Words for Chauncey

Controversial party leader and railroad magnate Chauncey Depew once attended a dinner where President William Howard Taft sat close by. Depew looked at Taft's mammoth 350-pound frame and sarcastically asked what he intended to call the child when it was born. Taft gave his tormentor a look and replied, "If it's a girl, I shall name her for my wife. If it's a boy, I shall call him Junior. But if it is, as I suspect, just gas, I will call it Chauncey Depew."

Ghostwriters?

Seating arrangements at Presidential news conferences are assigned to reporters so the Chief Executive can call on some of the journalists by name. In January of 1983, President Reagan pointed to the audience and called out the name "Bob Thompson." The room fell silent as television cameras searched for Mr. Thompson. But he wasn't there; in fact he was at home watching the press conference on television. A moment later the President pointed to another section of the audience and called "Al." There was no "Al" either, but another reporter alertly stood up and asked a question.

How About Some Heat?

Moving into the newly-constructed Executive Mansion in the fall of 1800, President John Adams found the mansion cold and foreboding. He recorded, "Not one room or chamber is finished of the whole. It is habitable by fires in every part, thirteen of which we are obliged to keep daily, or sleep in wet and damp places. But this House is built for ages to come."

He Doesn't Care

Following World War I, President Wilson went to Paris to convince the victorious allies that a League of Nations would prevent future wars. After his triumphant reception, Wilson soon grew tired of the petty jealousies and bickering among European leaders. World leaders argued and made impossible demands, and the President referred to Britain's Lloyd George and France's Clemenceau as "madmen." In a fit of frustration, he yelled to his doctor, "Logic! Logic! I don't give a damn for logic!" No doubt this sounded ironic coming from a former college professor.

No Time for Sergeants

Before boarding the Presidential plane at McCoy Air Force Base near Orlando, Florida, President Richard Nixon decided to meet some of the crowd gathered at the airport. It was evening and bright lights were shining in his eyes as he shook hands and held babies. Nixon noticed a young boy and a shadowy figure at the youth's side. As Nixon squinted to get a better look, he asked the adult beside the child, "Are you this boy's mother or grandmother?" Came the reply from Master Sergeant Edward Kleizo, "Neither." Nixon looked closer and said, "Of course not," then reached up and slapped the sergeant in the face. A couple of reporters witnessed the incident, and the next day millions of readers learned about it. Kleizo was questioned about what happened and told newsmen that it was just an affectionate slap and added, "I may not even wash my face again."

Man of Action

Zachary Taylor technically fought in four wars, the only President to do so. He served in the War of 1812, the Black Hawk War, the Seminole War, and the Mexican War.

The Lady in Red

Howard Chandler Christy, world renowned illustrator, painted portraits of several Presidents, First Ladies, and foreign dignitaries. He was asked to paint a full length portrait of Grace Coolidge. Christy suggested she wear a dark red gown, to contrast with their white-haired collie, which was also in the portrait. The First Lady, however, had no red gown and when she mentioned this to the President, Coolidge quipped, "Why not dye the dog red?"

78

In August of 1981 Ronald and Nancy Reagan stayed at their California ranch for nearly a month, secluded from cameras and news reporters. Reagan then decided to call an impromptu news conference to sign a tax and budget bill. He informed the reporters, "This is the first morning we haven't ridden. We decided instead that we'd come out and be ridden."

Pierced

When supporters of candidate Franklin Pierce tried to impress the public with their candidate's Mexican War record, one of little or no distinction, the Whigs published a one-inch tall book entitled "The Military Services of General Pierce." He was described as "a hero of many a well-fought *bottle*."

Macho Men?

Presidents Van Buren and Carter have both been accused of being sissies or effeminate. On the floor of Congress, President Van Buren was berated for using the same perfume as Queen Victoria.

Good Advice

Harry Truman voiced: "Three things can ruin a man — money, power, and women. I never had any money, I never wanted power, and the only woman in my life is up at the house right now."

Floundering Father?

Teddy Roosevelt told Henry Cabot Lodge in 1884 that George Washington was "the greatest of Americans." Roosevelt was also a great admirer of Lincoln, but his view of Thomas Jefferson was quite different. He regarded the third President as "the most incapable executive that ever filled the Presidential chair."

Todd, Almighty!

In referring to the reputation and social standing of his wife's family, Lincoln jokingly said, "God had only one 'd,' but there were two 'd's' in Todd." Mrs. Lincoln did not find the comment very amusing.

Rejected With No Regrets

Two years in a row George Bush's Yale baseball team reached the finals of the N.C.A.A. World Series. In 1947, Yale lost to the University of California, who was aided by future major league star Jackie Jensen. The following year, Yale won the eastern regional title again to advance to the World Series, only to lose to Southern Cal. The Trojans' batboy was Sparky Anderson, who later managed the Reds and Tigers to championships in the big leagues. Bush had high hopes of playing in the majors. He fielded well at first base, batted .280 his senior year, and established a reputation for hitting the long ball. No offers came. Though dejected over two consecutive losses in the collegiate World Series, and having been "overlooked" by big league scouts, the young team captain had no regrets. He did have the honor of meeting Babe Ruth in one of the Hall of Famer's last public appearances. Giving up his idea to pursue a baseball career, Bush worked hard to become a successful oilman.

Taken Literally

On Inauguration Day in 1893, President and Mrs. Benjamin Harrison suggested to their Indiana and Ohio friends that they would welcome callers at the White House. For the next three days, thousands of Midwesterners flocked to the mansion. The crush of visitors became so great the White House doors had to be bolted until guards could restore order. Harrison remarked that he had "probably shaken the hands of 8,000 persons since daylight." Executive business stood at a standstill, as the reception line each day seemed neverending. Thus, a friendly, casual, well-meaning remark of hospitality caused considerable inconvenience. But what followed was just as bad when office-seekers inundated the President. Harrison could not escape this horde either, and remained at his post several weeks to bring order out of chaos.

Is He Talking About U.S.?

George Washington had a rather dim view of his countrymen when he wrote from Boston in 1775, "The head of our armed forces declared that if he had known the depths of America's moral decay he would never have accepted his command." The commander further announced, "Such a dearth of public spirit and want of virtue, and fertility in all low acts to obtain advantages of one kind of another, I never saw before and hope I may never be witness to again."

All in the Family

Not all of our Presidents were indifferent to Indians. Thomas Jefferson once told a group of Miamis and Potawotomies, "Made by the same Great Spirit, and living in the same land with our brothers, the redmen, we consider ourselves as the same family; we wish to live with them as one people, and to cherish their interests as our own."

One is a Lonely Number

Henry W. Halleck was commander of the northern armies for a while during the Civil War. Disdainful, aloof, energetic, and highly intelligent, he proved to be a poor military leader. President Lincoln once said he was Halleck's friend because nobody else was.

Dog-gone

President Eisenhower banned his dog, Heidi, from the White House for urinating on the carpet of the Diplomatic Reception Room. Heidi spent the rest of her days at the Eisenhower farm at Gettysburg.

The Bare Facts

A friend once drove Congressman John F. Kennedy to Washington, D.C. It was quite warm in the car, so JFK took off his clothes — all of them.

Forget the Book and Take a Look

While Lincoln lived in Springfield, Illinois in the 1850's, he supposedly was pushing Tad in a baby carriage with one hand and holding an open book in the other. The baby fell out and was left behind as Lincoln strolled on, unaware of what happened. Lincoln was terribly absent-minded, and his wife constantly reminded him of important matters regarding appointments, dress, and duties.

Horse Sense

It was quite a big responsiblity for twelve-year-old Ulysses Grant to be driving a team of horses from Georgetown, Ohio to Cincinnati to haul goods. The young boy never had a problem, and years later when he was asked why his horse never stalled, Grant replied, "Because I never got stalled myself."

Let's Put It Another Way

President Teddy Roosevelt's policy of expansionism and Yankee imperialism was a reflection of his character. At a cabinet meeting he once explained the American - sponsored revolution in Central America and the recognition of the Republic of Panama, resulting in a treaty authorizing the construction of a canal there. He asked the cabinet members whether he had satisfactorily explained his actions. Secretary of War Elihu Root replied, "You certainly have, Mr. President. You have shown that you were accused of seduction and have conclusively proved that you were guilty of rape."

Not Much Left

In the fall of 1850 showman P.T. Barnum "struck gold" when he arranged a U.S. concert for singer Jenny Lind. In December he and the "Swedish Nightingale" were ushered into the White House where an anxious President and Mrs. Fillmore awaited a private performance. Miss Lind was somewhat nervous but was soon put at ease by the President's suggestion about places she should see in Washington. She summoned the courage to ask Fillmore, "How are the American people governed? I have heard much about your democracy, but I know little about the way it is performed." Fillmore smiled and replied, "Our people govern themselves, mostly, which does not leave much for the President to do."

Words to Live By

Abraham Lincoln penned these words of wisdom: "If I were to try to read, much less answer, all the attacks made on me this shop might as well be closed for any business. I do the very best I know how — the very best I can; and I mean to keep on doing so until the end. If the end brings me out all right, what is said against me won't amount to anything. If the end brings me out wrong, ten angels swearing I was right would make no difference." President William Howard Taft had this quotation photographed and framed for his office desk.

A Badmouthing Which Backfired

In 1884 ex-Congressman William McKinley campaigned for Presidential candidate James G. Blaine. At one debate an opponent claimed the Republican Party had rigged the economic structure so that any fool could get rich. Always proper and polite, McKinley was also quick with the wit. He calmly enquired of the claim, "Permit me to inquire further, Doctor, why you are not a wealthy man?" The roar of the crowd silenced the opponent.

A Man Who Prays, Not Preys

Following the great Union victories at Gettysburg and Vicksburg in early July of 1863, President Lincoln went to a Washington hospital to visit General Dan Sickles, who had been seriously wounded at Gettysburg. Sickles asked Lincoln if he had had any doubts about the outcome of the battle. Lincoln explained that many people, including his cabinet members, were apprehensive, but that *he* was confident. The President told Sickles that after going into his room, "I locked the door, and got down on my knees before Almighty God, and prayed to Him mightily for victory at Gettysburg. I told Him that this was His war, and our cause His cause, but we couldn't stand another Fredericksburg or Chancellorsville." Lincoln, in fact, spent much time praying. According to a White House usher, he spent an hour each morning in prayer, usually beginning around 4:00 a.m.

Let Me Clarify That

During the 1960 Democratic Convention Lyndon Johnson was asked about the possibility of sharing the national ticket with John F. Kennedy. He confided to Clare Booth Luce, "Honey, no way will I ever join that son of a bitch!" Later at the inaugural ball, Johnson explained to her, "Clare, I looked it up. One out of every four Presidents has died in office. I'm a gambling man, darlin', and this is the only chance I got."

Close Call

During the early part of the Civil War a tall man wearing a stovepipe hat showed up at the outskirts of Washington to examine fortifications. Rebel sharpshooters a few hundred yards away took aim at the stranger. A bullet whizzed by the man, leading a young soldier to yell, "Get down, you fool!" The target was President Lincoln, and the soldier screaming the order was Oliver Wendell Holmes. Lincoln took the advice and returned to the White House.

An Autograph Collector's Prize

There is no known signature of one of our President's wives — Hannah

Van Buren. Not even a facsimile of her signature is known to exist. She was never a First Lady, having died before her husband, Martin, became President.

A Second Chance

The wildest Presidential first-ball pitch in baseball has to go to Ronald Reagan. On Opening Day in 1986 at Baltimore's Memorial Stadium, the President stepped onto the field to perform the ritual. Having once portrayed Hall of Famer Grover Cleveland Alexander in the film "The Winning Team," this seemed like a simple task. With thousands watching, Reagan peered at catcher Rick Dempsey and uncorked a wild throw which sailed over Dempsey's head ten feet to the far right. The crowd roared with laughter, and Reagan asked for a second chance. His second pitch was a strike. Nearby media and fans breathed a sigh of relief.

For Cryin' Out Loud

The spectators and officials gathered in the House of Representatives to witness history in the making. It was George Washington's last day as

President. John Adams, the incoming President had to feel a bit uneasy, as he wrote in his diary, "There was more weeping than there has ever been at the representation of any tragedy."

Jimmy's Commandment

During the 1976 Presidential primaries Jimmy Carter voiced, "I'll never tell a lie." One of his campaign workers said sarcastically, "We're gonna lose the liar vote!" But Miss Lillian, Carter's mother, prevented any such thing from happening when she told reporters, "Well, I lie all the time. I have to — to balance the ticket!"

Kitchen Commander

Calvin Coolidge was not only a man of few words, he was also a man of thrift. He personally initialed all bills and questioned what he felt was extravagance in purchasing food or supplies for the White House. He even inspected the White House kitchen to see how much food was being used. After leaving office, he was once asked what his greatest disappointment was, and he reportedly said that it was his inability to find out what was happening to the leftovers.

I Didn't Know You Cared

Lincoln's mail following his election was overwhelming. The President-elect received several portraits by noted artists. In January of 1861, the Lincolns were presented a painting from South Carolina in which a rebel artist depicted the "Railsplitter" with chained feet, a rope around his neck, and a coating of tar and feathers on his long body.

Just for Mom

It was President Woodrow Wilson who made Mother's Day a recognized special event. This was in 1914, and Wilson declared that red carnations should be worn in memory of deceased mothers and white ones for the living.

Give and Take — and Give

Only one American in history has had the Medal of Honor taken away and then restored. This was a woman, Dr. Mary E. Walker. Dr. Walker was rather persistent, for during the Civil War she demanded to be treated like a doctor, not a nurse. She also badgered Army personnel and government officials for an increase in pay and rank. Dr. Walker not only served at four major battles, she also worked as a Union spy, and was captured by Confederate forces in 1864. She spent four months in Libby Prison, using her surgical skills to help the sick and wounded.

Following her release, she demanded back pay as an Army officer, but was offered much less that what she asked. Taking her case before President Andrew Johnson, the War Department, and Congress, she agreed to cease her demands if she would be given the rank of major. Instead, the government presented her with the Medal of Honor for conspicuous bravery, to the detriment of her own health, and for aid to soldiers on the battlefield and in hospitals. For the next twenty-five years, she continued her attacks, insisting on a pension and more recognition of her services. She also became actively involved in women's rights, much to the consternation of many government officials.

Even more damaging were her remarks a few days after McKinley's assassination. At the train station in Oswego, New York, she told a small group of people, "The state of New York if it electrocutes the assassin of McKinley is just as great a murderer as he is. President McKinley was a murderer because he killed the poor Filipinos." Only cooler heads prevented Dr. Walker from being beaten and hanged. Then in 1916, a special commission under Woodrow Wilson declared her medal unwarranted. Not until 1977 was it restored.

De-parting Shot

On a night in August of 1861, Lincoln was riding his horse along a dark street. Suddenly a shot rang out and the horse and rider sped away, leaving the President's stovepipe hat behind. The next day, Lincoln's hat was discovered with a bullet hole right through the top. Lincoln found the incident amusing and often told the story to friends.

Out of Tune

"The Missouri Waltz" was *NOT* Harry Truman's favorite song. He hated it, and once when President Richard Nixon played it on the piano for him, the elderly Truman made some highly critical remarks about the song and *the piano player.*

Arthur's Absence

President Chester Arthur officially opened the World's Industrial Exposition in New Orleans — and he wasn't even there! Via electrical wire connecting Washington and New Orleans, he pushed a button which set the machinery in motion. This was in December of 1884.

Nature's Salute

In June of 1984 President Reagan toured the United Kingdom. While visiting Ireland, he was met with mild protests, rain and a hail storm. The press described this part of the President's journey as "hail to the chief."

A Battle of "Bunker Bill"

President Taft took up golf to work out some of his frustrations, but sometimes it got the best of him. According to an aide, "The President no longer is philosophical when he plays badly. The other day he swore a terrific oath (after a bad shot) and threw his club 25 yards." Taft once took *nineteen shots* to get out of a bunker. He and Gerald Ford would have made quite a twosome!

Labor vs. Capital

U.S. Grant said, "Whatever there is of greatness in the United States, or indeed in any other country, is due to labor. The laborer is the author of all greatness and wealth. Without labor there would be no government, and no leading class, and nothing to preserve." Abraham Lincoln said, "Labor is the superior of capital."

Twister-Proof

The most destructive tornado ever to hit Ohio roared through the city of Xenia on April 3, 1974. The historic Xenia Hotel was almost completely destroyed except for one large piece of Presidential memorabilia which remained intact and unscratched, the William McKinley bed in which the 25th President once slept.

Betty's Coattails

In the 1976 Presidential campaign thousands of Republican supporters wore buttons proclaiming "Betty's husband for President." Gerald Ford was flattered, but lost the election to Jimmy Carter.

Staking His Life On It

Said Lincoln on the way to his first inauguration under the threat of assassination, "If this country cannot be saved without giving up the principle of equal rights, I would rather be assassinated than surrender . . . I have said nothing but what I am willing to live by, and if it be the pleasure of Almighty God, to die by."

Fit For a King

Incumbent Martin Van Buren was severely criticized by the Whig Party when it was learned he had installed a bathtub in the White House. The Whigs, who were promoting William Henry Harrison for the Presidency, accused him of seeking pleasures "of a palace life."

Give Due Account to the Count

John F. Kennedy is often quoted as having said, "Victory finds a hundred fathers, but defeat is an orphan." He did say this following the debacle at the Bay of Pigs invasion in April of 1961. But his remark belongs to Count Galeazzo Ciano, who recorded it in his diary in 1942.

Stamp of Disapproval

George Washington, at the suggestion of John Adams, was unanimously elected Commander-in-Chief of the Continental Army. Obliged to serve, Washington had not desired or sought the position. Upon learning of his new office, he remarked to Patrick Henry, "This day will be the commencement of the decline of my reputation."

Elections Sinking to a New Low

The townspeople of Emmitsburg, Iowa have a unique way of measuring a Presidential candidate's popularity. After a candidate's name is announced, the citizens there flush their toilets for their favorite contender. The number of flushes is measured in the water tower level. The candidate with the lowest measurable water pressure usually proves to be the winner in Iowa's race. As much as 19,000 gallons of water may be used. One farmer remarked that the Des Moines River rose three feet during the "survey." It has also been said that the winning candidates are often "flushed with pride."

Bad Lad Tad

Lincoln rarely showed any anger to his son's behavior. Tad was often insolent, interrupting and boisterous, but his father demonstrated great patience. On one occasion, however, the President lost his temper. Once, while Lincoln was reviewing troops from the White House portico, young Tad stood behind him waving a Confederate flag. Lincoln detected some hostility in the crowd, and when he turned around, grabbed the youth and roughly handed him to an aide. Tad thought the gesture was amusing, but father felt otherwise.

Evicted

During part of his second term, James Madison had no Executive Mansion. The British burned it, and he and Dolley lived in a home at Pennsylvania Avenue and Nineteenth Street known as "The House of a Thousand Candles."

In God We Trust?

Three Presidents have been sworn in without the use of a *Holy Bible* — Thomas Jefferson, Theodore Roosevelt (in 1901), and Lyndon Johnson (in 1963). Johnson was sworn in with John Kennedy's Catholic missal (mass book) aboard *Air Force One* following Kennedy's assassination in Dallas. Incidentally, federal law does not stipulate that the *Holy Bible* be used for such a ceremony.

A Boy's Best Years

On the subject of boyhood, Herbert Hoover once told some dinner guests, "The eyes of all ten-year-old Iowa boys are or should be filled with the wonders of Iowa's streams and woods, of the mystery of growing crops. His days should be filled with adventure and great undertakings, with participation in good and comforting things."

A Prayer and a Plea

James Buchanan's untamed spirit led to his dismissal from Dickinson College. But his family minister pleaded with school officials and the young Pennsylvanian was reinstated later, graduating with highest honors.

Garfield's Goodies

In 1880 eight-year-old Calvin Coolidge asked his father for a penny to buy some candy. Papa refused, explaining that if a Democrat was elected hard times would follow and every penny would be needed. Garfield, however, narrowly defeated his Democratic opponent Winfield Hancock, and young Cal got his candy.

Standing Room Only

In 1984 President Reagan held a dinner in honor of former French President Vale'ry Giscard d'Estaing. Following the banquet, the President and First Lady accompanied the Frenchman and his wife to some entertainment. Reagan, walking arm-in-arm with Mrs. d'Estaing, motioned for her to sit down, but she did not move. Not able to speak French, Reagan again gestured to his guest to sit down, but she remained standing. The President then summoned a translator and informed him to tell Mrs. d'Estaing to please be seated. Then came the reply, "I can't. You're standing on my dress."

Many people know that Abraham Lincoln was assassinated while watching the performance of the popular play "Our American Cousin" at Ford's Theater in Washington, D.C. But that same play was also running in Chicago at the McVerick Theater on the day Lincoln was nominated for President in that city.

The Boss's Daughter

Frank Pierce, our fourteenth President, was not a good student his first couple years at Bowdoin College, but he did pass, as well as make passes. He fell in love with Jane Appleton, daughter of the college's president. They were married ten years after Frank's graduation.

Reason to Celebrate

Eleanor Roosevelt was married to Franklin on St. Patrick's Day, which was also her mother's birthday. And everyone knows that her Uncle Teddy, the 26th President, attended the event to give away the bride.

A View From the Top

LBJ was reportedly quite a ladies' man. While visiting Australia in 1966, he met and became friends with Prime Minister Harold Holt and his wife. Mrs. Holt was an attractive, shapely woman with a great sense of humor. The President once put his arm around Mrs. Holt's shoulder and stared into the plunging neckline of her dress. Then, clapping his hands together, he turned to the Prime Minister with a grin and said, "Harold, you sure know how to pick 'em." Lady Bird fixed a disapproving glare, but Mrs. Holt simply tossed back her head and laughed.

Arrogant Abe

Once Abraham Lincoln made up his mind about something, no power on earth could change it. It was during the Civil War that Senator Fessenden made the following critical remarks: "You cannot change the President's character or conduct, unfortunately; he remained long enough at Springfield, surrounded by toadies and office-seekers, to persuade himself that he was specially chosen by the Almighty for this crisis, and well chosen. This conceit has never been beaten out of him."

Ah, Wilderness

When President Jimmy Carter vacationed in the Grand Tetons of Wyoming in 1978, NBC spent more that $50,000 just to transmit the story from the wilderness to "Nightly News" headquarters in New York. In addition, the television company sent along three correspondents, three producers, and two camera crews.

Even Me?

It was 1864, and Vice President-elect Andrew Johnson was in Nashville. It was reported that Confederate General Hood was advancing on the city. Union Commander Wilson, in dire need of horses for his army, impounded all horses in the region. Among those "drafted" were a couple of Andy Johnson's best horses.

Win Some, Lose Some

In three Presidential elections John Quincy Adams failed to win a majority in both popular and electoral votes! Yet he became President in 1824 when the House of Representatives decided the election. Incidentally, in 1820, Adams received only one electoral vote to Monroe's 231. And in 1824, Andrew Jackson beat him soundly in the popular vote, but could not win a majority of electors. Then in 1828, Adams failed in his bid for re-election, losing to "Old Hickory."

There Is A Difference

President Kennedy once remarked, "An error doesn't become a mistake unless one intends to conceal it." This quote followed the Bay of Pigs fiasco where the President failed to provide promised air support to pro-American Cubans when they invaded Castro's island nation.

Copy Cat

George Washington commissioned the French architect Pierre L'Enfant to design a capital for the United States. The planning and construction of the city inspired another country to plan its capital in a similar fashion. Thus, the only foreign capital modeled after our own is that of Canberra, Australia.

What A Trip!

In the summer of 1852 a young Army officer, his regiment, and their families left New York for the Oregon Territory. Sailing south, these Americans crossed the narrow isthmus of Panama by land, since there was no canal at the time. Torrents of rain, blinding sun, and hot, steamy jungles combined with mosquitoes and disease to meet the group. Army mules, which were supposed to carry passengers and supplies, were never delivered. Cholera and typhoid took 37 lives the first day. Watching panic seize his ranks, the young quartermaster rounded up natives to transport the sick in hammocks. He stayed behind to attend to the very ill and bury the dead. A hundred more died, but the officer remained calm and worked several days without sleep. Finally, he staggered into Panama City, regrouped his decimated army, and headed north to their destination. In his letter home to his family, the officer made no mention of the terrible ordeal they had encountered. Yet those with him never forgot his superhuman effort and determination to save the remaining men, women, and children. And only a few history books note that this young quartermaster was none other than Ulysses S. Grant.

A Taste for Travel

President Grover Cleveland and his Chinese cook introduced chop suey to Americans. One hundred years earlier, Thomas Jefferson had brought back the idea of French fries while ambassador to France. Oh, I almost forgot — Jefferson also introduced spaghetti in 1787.

Catatonic Mac

Tired of hearing excuses by General George McClellan, and tired of his inactivity during the Civil War, Lincoln sent the General the following message, "If you don't want to use the army, I should like to borrow it for a while."

Bloody Prank

Of all the practical jokes Ronald Reagan ever played, he was most proud of the stunt he organized as a sophomore at Eureka College. He staged an evening watermelon hunt to make several lowly freshmen believe they had witnessed a shooting. As the students tiptoed through the watermelon patch at a prearranged location, the place exploded in light. A shotgun blast went off and an upperclassman near Reagan screamed and collapsed, gripping his chest and red fluid flowing through his fingers. "I'm shot," he screamed. "My God, I *am* shot." The horrified students were sent on foot eight miles back to town to find a doctor. When the authorities learned of this, Reagan explained he was merely a bystander. Reagan and his fraternity brothers each paid the doctor ten dollars, minimizing the prank.

The Lincoln Lion

Lincoln was arguing a case for a farmer one day in an Illinois court. An old judge corrected Lincoln's pronounciation of the word "lien." The judge wrongly suggested that the world should be pronounced as "lion" not "lean." Lincoln did not argue and went on with his remarks. In a minute he used the word again saying it his way, and again the judge corrected him. Lincoln used the word again, pronouncing it properly, whereupon the judge, by now a bit agitated, told him to say it "lion." Finally, Lincoln looked at the judge and replied, "As you please, your honor, if my client had known there was a lion on his farm he wouldn't have stayed there long enough to bring this suit."

It Happened Anyway

Harry Truman was questioned whether he would like serving under FDR as Vice President. He felt the office was ceremonial, commenting to a Missouri friend, "I have no ambitions to run for any office but United State Senator. A fellow is just a figurehead when he gets to be Vice President of the United States. He is merely sitting around waiting for a funeral, and I don't like funerals."

Some Hope for Ford

Bob Hope described Gerald Ford as "The Man Who Made Golf a Contact Sport." Gerald Ford gained a reputation as an erratic hitter, beaning skulls and backsides of anyone within 260 yards. Here are some lines from Hope's book on golf: "Ford doesn't have to keep score. He can just look back and count the walking wounded. He drives well, too. He's never lost a golf cart yet. You all know Jerry Ford — the most dangerous driver since Ben Hur. Ford is easy to spot on the course; he drives the cart with the red cross painted on top. Whenever I play him, I usually try to make it a foursome — the President, myself, a paramedic and a faith healer." Hope added that Ford once took his golf ball out of the cup, threw it to the gallery and missed. He also added that Ford's Secret Service agents demand combat pay.

Words for Wee Ones

Tad Lincoln's playmates often provided light moments for Papa. One small girl playing with the President's large pocket watch asked him if it could be broken. "Of course it can't. Why, little girl, you hit it as hard as you can with a bunch of wool and even that won't break it." Another time he asked a young boy several questions the lad enjoyed answering. Lincoln patted him on the shoulder and sent him away with a puzzling but pleasant remark, "Well, you'll be a man before your mother . . ." Such incidents demonstrated his love and compassion for children.

Free Advice

In 1798 George Washington complained to his dentist, John Greenwood, that the dentures he had made for him were discolored. Returning the teeth, Greenwood advised him that the stains were "occasioned either by your soaking them in port-wine, or drinking it. Port, being sour, takes off all the polish . . . I advise you to either take them out after drinks and put them in clear water and put in another set, or clean them with a brush and some chalk finely scraped."

Abe was Apprehended

As a young man Abraham Lincoln was arrested. A competing ferryboat company from Kentucky claimed he violated the law in that his ferryboat ran across the middle of the river. Lincoln was a resident of Indiana. The judge hearing the case disagreed on the charge and the future President was allowed to continue carrying passengers and livestock across. This case had special significance because it got him thinking about the law. By reading legal books on his own he became an expert lawyer.

A Little Hypocrisy

During two different campaigns Richard Nixon expressed mixed feelings about college students. At Cornell University in 1956, during a question and answer period, he remarked to an aide, "Get me away from these little monsters." But while campaigning in 1968, he told a newspaper reporter in Oregon, "I always like to see college kids. I'm trying to get into college myself — the electoral college."

Rebel Rebuff Remembered

It was during the Mexican War that a young lieutenant rode his horse to General Winfield Scott's headquarters. The general's top aide, Colonel Robert E. Lee, informed the dirty, sloppily-dressed lieutenant that all officers reporting to headquarters should be neatly attired in full uniform. But the young officer would forever be a poor example of military fashion — his name was Ulysses S. Grant. Years later when the two juggernauts met at Appomattox, Lee could not recall the incident, but Grant never forgot it.

Remember Me?

In the first week of his new administration FDR called his Secretary of Labor, Frances Perkins. An assistant at the Department of Labor picked up the phone and heard a voice say, "This is Frank. May I speak to Miss Perkins?" The assistant relayed the message, but Miss Perkins inquired, "Frank? I don't know any Frank. Ask him whom he's with." Questioned, the caller chuckled and stated, "With the United States. This is the President."

Preaching Non-Stop

James Garfield's preaching did not cease when the Civil War began. An ordained minister of the Campbellites (Disciples of Christ), the future President preached in many churches before and during the war. While his regiment was stationed in Alabama, Garfield conducted worship services for the troops. In Mooresville, a small town six miles south of Decatur, Garfield preached at least two sermons. A plaque commemorates the event. Even during his Congressional years, he occasionally preached sermons to eager congregations.

Maybe He Didn't Know

President Reagan was constantly criticized for his lack of detail and being uninformed of important information. In a bit of self-mockery, he once explained his stand on armament and defense spending by noting, "I've been getting some flack about ordering the production of the B-1 bomber. How did I know it was an airplane? I thought it was a vitamin for the troops."

Views on a War

U. S. Grant's views on the Mexican War were different than his views on the War Between the States. He felt the Mexican War was unjustified, and added that America lost five times as many soldiers to disease and accidents as to Mexican bullets. Grant wrote, "My regiment lost four commissioned officers, all senior to me, by steamboat explosions. The Mexicans were not so discriminating. They sometimes picked off my juniors."

Do It My Way, Doc!

When Dwight Eisenhower was in the eighth grade, he fell down and, along with tearing a new pair of trousers, cut his knee. Soon his knee swelled as blood poisoning set in. Matters got worse as the infection spread. A doctor was summoned and, after taking one look, drew a line above the knee advising amputation to save the boy's leg.

The youngster shook his head — he would not allow it. He said he would rather die than live as a cripple. His parents, deeply religious who always taught their children individual responsibility and faith, left the decision up to Ike. For the next two weeks, the swelling increased. The entire leg turned black. The doctor called in a specialist from Topeka, and both men decided that amputation was urgent if the patient was to live. Ike still refused.

As the pain became unbearable, Ike felt he was going to pass out, so he called his brother Edgar to his side and made him promise not to let the physicians cut off his leg. Edgar agreed, and for the next fifteen days, he stood guard over him or slept near the doorway to Ike's bedroom. But the infection continued to spread and the leg swelled to twice its normal size. It began smelling terribly and oozing pus.

The doctor told the parents it would be murder not to operate, but Mama Eisenhower prayed and left the decision up to her son. That evening Edgar stood by because Ike feared the doctors would sneak in and operate. The next morning the boys noticed that the color in the leg had faded. Weeks later the swelling receded, and the crisis ended. Ike's recovery was slow, and he missed so much school that he had to repeat eighth grade. The courage, determination and independence young Eisenhower demonstrated were characteristics which made him a great soldier and President of the United States.

Is That So?

These days when the President and First Lady sponsor the annual Easter egg hunt on the White House lawn, more than 35,000 people show up.

Said Dwight Eisenhower, "As quickly as you start spending the taxpayer's money in large amounts, it looks like free money."

Thomas Jefferson wrote his own edition of the New Testament (written in four languages). This valuable edition is now in the Smithsonian Institution.

John Quincy Adams described Andrew Jackson as a "barbarian who could not write a sentence of grammar and hardly spell his own name."

Ulysses S. Grant and Grover Cleveland were distant cousins.

In his last public address, Abraham Lincoln told a crowd of listeners, "Important principles may and must be inflexible."

The first person to officially walk across the Brooklyn Bridge when it was completed in 1883 was the President of the United States — Chester A. Arthur.

Said Theodore Roosevelt, "No man is worth his salt who is not ready at all times to risk his body . . . to risk his well-being . . . to risk his life . . . in a great cause."

Jimmy Carter's nickname as a teenager was "Hot Shot."

In 1952, one newspaper commented that Dwight D. Eisenhower was known for his generalities, describing him as "the extremely General Eisenhower."

Advice from Andrew Jackson: "Take time to deliberate; but when the time for action arrives, stop thinking and go on."

The Secret Service's code name for Ronald Reagan was "Rawhide."

Ulysses S. Grant's only wish after graduating from West Point was to become a math teacher.

On August 6, 1945 President Harry Truman announced to the world that an atomic bomb had been used against the people of Japan at Hiroshima. In an eloquent sentence, he said, "The force upon which the sun draws its power has been loosed against those who brought war to the Far East."

In 1837, the New Hampshire legislature elected Frank Pierce as U.S. Senator. The future President was only 33 years old at the time.

James Monroe said in his first inaugural address, "National honor is the national property of the highest value."

Richard Nixon set aside every Wednesday for "think time," when he spent a session in solitude inside the White House.

William McKinley's pet parrot often whistled "Yankee Doodle."

Abe Lincoln read all of *Aesop's Fables* several times and had them memorized.

Thomas Jefferson reflected, "I would rather be shut up in a very modest cottage with my books, my family and a few old friends, dining on simple bacon and letting the world roll by as it liked, than to occupy the most splendid post which any human power can give."

President James Polk demanded that his cabinet members submit monthly reports on the performance of their clerks.

Benjamin Harrison's cold and dignified approach to politics made him few friends. Lacking personality, his formal attitude was devoid of humor. Harrison described his life "about as barren of anything funny as the Great Desert of grass."

When President John Tyler, a 54-year-old widower, married Julia Gardiner (only 24) it was quite a romance. Julia's younger sister felt compelled to warn her: "You spend so much time in kissing, things of more importance are left undone."

Not only was James Madison the "Father of the Constitution," he was also the designer of the Bill of Rights. His main priorities were guaranteeing freedom of the press, right to assemble and religious freedom.

When a White House cook could not figure out how to work a newly invented stove, President Fillmore went to the U.S. Patent Office, inspected the plans and taught his cook how to use it.

William Henry Harrison introduced celery, turnips and radishes to the people of Colombia. For a brief period he served as ambassador to this South American country, having taken a packet of garden seeds from the banks of the Ohio River.

Martin Van Buren was probably the first President to regulate working conditions when he decreed that "no person should labor more than ten hours a day in federal public works."

In 1840, Presidential candidate William Henry Harrison said in a speech: "All the measures of the Government are directed to the purpose of making the rich richer and the poor poorer."

In 1960, while Ronald Reagan was hosting TV's "G.E.Theater," he and his wife starred in an episode entitled "A Turkey for the President."

Eight Presidents are buried in state capitals.

Harry Truman saw an epitaph in the cemetery at Tombstone, Arizona, which described his feelings about his entire career: "Here lies Jack Williams. He done his Damndest."

Calvin Coolidge said, "Knowledge comes, but wisdom lingers."

Andrew Jackson read only one book of fiction during his life. It was a novel entitled *The Vicar of Wakefield*.

Years after retiring from the Presidency, John Tyler was in bad financial straits, so he went to the Bank of the United States for a loan. He was turned down.

Abraham Lincoln once said, "My father taught me how to work, but not to love it. I never did like work and I admit it. I'd rather read, tell stories, crack jokes, talk, laugh — anything but work."

No President has been born in June or died in May.

"A man must fulfill his destiny." So said John Quincy Adams.

Quipped FDR, "There is nothing I love so much as a good fight."

Thomas Jefferson once said, "Liberties are lost because people are too lazy to read the law closely."

In a 1982 survey of American historians, James Garfield was the only Chief Executive from Ohio (there were eight) who ranked above average. He was categorized as the 15th most successful.

Regarding his White House staff, Lyndon Johnson said, "I'll get my action from the younger men and my advice from the older men."

In 1888, the President's salary was $50,000, and the Vice President received just $8,000.

Because he was President during the 1837 Depression, Martin Van Buren was referred to as Van *Ruin*.

James K. Polk was the oldest of ten children; yet he had none of his own. Consequently, there are no direct descendants of the eleventh President.

The first President to travel by jet while in office was Dwight Eisenhower.

Theodore Roosevelt pointed out that "no man is above the law and no man is below it."

Senator Henry Clay described Andrew Jackson as "ignorant, passionate, hypocritical, corrupt, and easily swayed by the base men who surround him."

During his campaign for the White House, Vice President George Bush noted that the greatest accomplishment he was proudest of the last forty years was "the fact that my children still come home."

One of our Presidents had his daughter appear in a movie with Elvis Presley. Ronald Reagan's daughter, Maureen, had a brief role in the 1964 film "Kissin' Cousins."

President Warren Harding once quipped, "I am not worried about my enemies; it is my friends that are keeping me awake nights."

Abraham Lincoln signed the first federal income tax into law — a three percent tax on income above $600.

Harry Truman was not much of a hunter. Said he, "I don't like to hunt animals and I never have. I do not believe in shooting at anything that cannot shoot back."

Thomas Jefferson considered the greatest men who ever lived to be Bacon, Newton, and Locke.

James Madison and Zachary Taylor, second cousins, were named after the same man — their great-grandfather, James Taylor of Virginia.

On the subject of Gerald Ford, actress Shirley MacLaine in 1976 said, "How can you dislike a guy who eats a tamale with the wrapper still on it?"

In 1981 a pair of George Washington's false teeth were stolen from the Smithsonian. The "choppers" were made of ivory set in gold.

While in office, Rutherford B. Hayes enjoyed traveling incognito. He would sit next to strangers or join in on informal conversations. He wore an old slouch hat and a black alpaca coat.

"Liberty with Power" was the motto of John Quincy Adams's administration.

George Washington appeared before the Senate to present a proposed treaty with the Creek Indians. After two days of bickering he left, declaring that he would be "damned" if he ever went there again. He never did, and succeeding Presidents followed suit.

Following the mid-term elections of 1858, President James Buchanan realized the Democrats had taken a beating. After big losses in the Congress, he wrote his niece, "We have met the enemy and we are theirs."

Grover Cleveland was a man of courage. Some historians feel he was the greatest President between Lincoln and Theodore Roosevelt. Former Democratic candidate Samuel J. Tilden once exclaimed, "Backbone! He has so much that it makes his stomach stick out front!"

John Kennedy met his future wife at a dinner party. As he explained, "I leaned over the asparagus and asked her for a date."

Nixon admitted that as a youth he was not hard to please. There was nothing he liked "better than a rich milkshake." Yet, because of his weight problem, he deprived himself of indulging in such pleasures.

Attending Harvard at the age of 15, John Adams learned that swearing was a five-shilling fine. And his breakfast consisted of bread and beer.

During dull moments of Congressional debate, James Garfield used his learning of Greek to translate odes of Horatio.

In a very unpopular decision, Franklin Pierce sent U.S. troops into Boston. A native New Englander, Pierce did this to assure the extradition of a runaway slave. Abolitionists and other anti-Southern groups felt betrayed and even made threats on Pierce's life.

The first President to address the Gridiron Club was Benjamin Harrison. Dispelling the perception that he was a humorless and distant person, Harrison told the group of journalists, " This is the second time this week that I have been called upon to open a congress of inventors."

Speaking at the Patent Office in 1900, President McKinley said, "Everything that can possibly be invented has already been invented."

As a lawyer on the circuit, Lincoln would often challenge other attorneys to a game of billiards.

Addressing the graduation class at Columbia University in 1889, President Cleveland said, "Sensible and responsible women will never want to vote."

In 1941, FDR wanted to create a national conservation institution in the name of President Benjamin Harrison, but World War II broke out and the idea was forgotten.

"Government, after all, is a very simple thing," quipped Warren Harding.

Following the autopsy on President James A. Garfield, doctors presented their patient's bullet-damaged vertebrae to the prosecution at the assassin's trial. Charles Guiteau, the murderer, handled these bones of his victim in the courtroom.

During his first trip to Europe, teenager Theodore Roosevelt read 50 novels.

Thomas Jefferson left us with this valuable piece of advice: "Neither believe nor reject anything because other persons ... rejected or believed it. Your own reason is the only oracle given you by heaven."

President Jimmy Carter's pilot on *Air Force One* (also dubbed "Peanut One") was Jimmy Carter. They were not related.

William McKinley said that "self preservation is the first law of nature, as it is and should be of nations."

Warren G. Harding was editor, publisher, and owner of the *Marion Star* newspaper when he was only 19.

All five children of Franklin and Eleanor Roosevelt got divorces after their marriages.

"Next in importance to freedom and justice is popular education, without which freedom nor justice can be permanently maintained." These were the words of a former teacher — James A. Garfield.

Let's eat! At the inaugural ball held in honor of James Buchanan, the food table was 250 feet long.

Woodrow Wilson once stated, "I use not only all the brains I have, but all I can borrow."

Chester A. Arthur was the first Phi Beta Kappa President.

Abraham Lincoln once asked, "If I was two-faced, would I be using this one?"

Chief Justice John Marshall administered the oath of office to Presidents on nine different occasions.

Prior to the American Revolution, George Washington told British superiors, "Honest men have the right to act on their conscience without being called rebels or traitors."

Teddy Roosevelt was President when the first World Series of baseball was played.

While John Quincy Adams was President the Congress allotted the White House a flock of sheep and two cows.

Dwight Eisenhower once said, "Any man who is not prepared to admit publicly he has been wrong is wrong." This statement followed the Russian capture of a U.S. spy plane as Francis Gary Powers was on an espionage mission.

Abraham Lincoln was a direct descendant of England's King Edward I, who had many physical similarities of the 16th President.

Ronald Reagan, not Humphrey Bogart, was originally cast for the title role in "Casablanca," one of Hollywood's all-time classic movies. Reagan appeared in 54 Hollywood films.

Public records show that Andrew Jackson was the first Presidential candidate handed a baby to kiss. Jackson promptly informed an aide to perform the task.

THIS IS NOT PART OF MY JOB DESCRIPTION!

Thomas Jefferson had a special place in his heart for farmers when he said, "Those who labor in the earth are the chosen people of God."

In 1984, WKRC-TV in Cincinnati canceled the movie "Knute Rockne - All American," starring Ronald Reagan. The management there felt that showing the film violated federal law regarding equal time for Presidential candidates.

The only candidate to run for Vice President on a losing ticket who later became President was FDR.

Only three man were defeated in a first attempt for the Presidency and then subsequently elected — William Henry Harrison, Andrew Jackson, and Richard Nixon.

President Taft found "Hail to the Chief" so distasteful he ordered the Marine Band not to play it.

On the morning of the D-Day Invasion, General Dwight Eisenhower visited British soldiers preparing for the assault. Having talked with other allied units the previous day, "Ike" wished the soldiers good fortune and God speed. And in his pocket he jingled three good-luck coins, one British, one French, and one American.

Herbert Hoover's strict Quaker upbringing forbade him to dance. He once explained to Reverend John J. Burke, "I cannot dance because of both my faith and my ignorance."

Harry Truman offered this advice for potential elected officials: "No young man should go into politics if he wants to get rich or if he expects an adequate reward for his services. An honest public servant can't expect to become rich in politics. He can only attain greatness and satisfaction by service."

While working in Mr. Rogers's law office in Buffalo, seventeen-year-old Grover Cleveland was accidentally locked in the building by the other clerks. Cleveland found the incident amusing and remarked, " Someday I shall be better remembered."

Just before he died, George Washington monitored his own faint and fading pulse.

The name "Nixon" is derived from two Irish words meaning "he faileth not." In his tenure of office, Nixon lacked the luck of the Irish.

Chester Arthur missed perfection by one point in college. Of the 79 students listed in the Union College class of 1848, ten of them had a perfect record of 500 grade points. Arthur got 499, and upon graduation, was elected to Phi Beta Kappa.

During his last few months in office Franklin Pierce realized he had been a failure. His friend and former college classmate, Nathaniel Hawthorne, wrote him, "Frank, I pity you — indeed I do from the bottom of my heart."

Surgeons J.J. Woodward and Edward Curtis performed the autopsy on Abraham Lincoln. And sixteen years later these two doctors also participated in the post-mortem examination of James A. Garfield.

President Benjamin Harrison signed a law establishing the Pledge of Allegiance.

At a 1986 New York autograph auction, a signed photograph by three former Presidents sold for $1,100. A picture was taken of Carter, Ford, and Nixon attending the funeral services in the Capitol for Senator and former Vice President Hubert Humphrey. Four years later it was priced at $3,000.

Three Roosevelts have held the post of Assistant Secretary of the Navy. Theodore, his son Theodore, Jr., and Franklin all served in the family tradition.

Woofer the Coyote (a small dog), Rebecca the Robot, and Bozo the Clown all ran for President in 1984. They were defeated by Ronald Reagan.

George Washington's first act as commander of the American forces was to protest the lack of outhouses for his men. In the encampment outside of Boston, he discovered a severe shortage of privies.

Three years after the Adamses moved in, the White House was still not completely built. In 1804, Thomas Jefferson found that the roof and gutters leaked so badly that the furniture had to be covered. There was no basement either, and the piles of rubbish and deep pits made the structure a most unattractive place.

"Unless each day can be looked upon by an individual as one in which he has had some fun, some joy, some real satisfaction, that day is a loss." — Dwight D. Eisenhower

On the battlefield in Resaca de la Palma, Mexico, a friendly camp peddler suggested to General Zachary Taylor that he was too close the the enemy. "Old Rough and Ready" replied (with sword in hand), "Let us ride a little nearer." Taylor's unorthodox, but gallant, leadership won him the hearts of his men and four major victories during the Mexican War.

Lamenting on a lack of privacy, Dwight Eisenhower remarked, "You know, once in a while I get to the point with everybody staring at me, where I want to go back indoors and pull down the curtains."

Ronald Reagan's favorite horse was Sinbad, his mount during his television series "Death Valley Days."

Thomas Jefferson had a rather negative viewpoint in regard to appointed government officeholders: "Few die and none resign."

John Quincy Adams was a gracious winner. Henry Clay became his Secretary of State — the same man he defeated for the Presidency. Critics claimed the two struck a bargain so Adams could defeat Andrew Jackson in the race for the White House.

Martin Van Buren's son, John, was asked to run for President in 1848 under the Free Soil banner. He refused, so his father accepted the nomination instead and lost to Zachary Taylor, our 12th Chief Executive.

Said Woodrow Wilson, "The President is at liberty both in law and in conscience, to be as big a man as he can."

Franklin D. Roosevelt was related to many famous people in England and the United States, and to some infamous ones too, including John Wilkes Booth, who murdered Abraham Lincoln.

James A. Garfield recorded in his diary that "Grant's imperturbability is amazing. I am in doubt whether to call it greatness or stupidity."

William Howard Taft was nicknamed "Big Lub" by his classmates at Yale.

Richard Nixon's favorite food? Cherry pie.

Though not generally known, Dr. Charles Leale used both mouth-to-mouth resuscitation and cardiac massage to revive Lincoln after he was shot at Ford's Theater. Leale's efforts, combined with removing a blood clot from the back of the victim's head, kept the President alive for another nine hours.

Ex-President Theodore Roosevelt was very disappointed that he did not receive a commission from President Wilson to lead troops during World War I. And he offered this advice to those who might have some misgivings about fighting: "You can't have peace without sacrifice. You can't have security without service."

Richard Nixon noted, "Life for everyone is a series of crises."

The day after the British burned the White House and many other buildings in the capital, a rare tornado swept through the city completing the destruction.

Warren G. Harding found it increasingly difficult to relax after learning of corruption in his administration, and he could not fall asleep except in a half-sitting position.

James Monroe, like Washington, scorned political parties. He considered them a "curse" and thought government should be based on "virtue."

Franklin Pierce said the only person he preferred talking politics with was former First Lady Sarah Polk.

As a college professor, Woodrow Wilson once wrote: "Men of ordinary physique and discretion cannot be Presidents and live, if the strain cannot be somehow relieved."

In 1961, Harry Truman told a friend, "Men don't change. The only thing new in the world is the history you don't know."

When Abraham Lincoln took his oath of office on March 4, 1861, five former Presidents and eleven future Presidents were alive.

Ronald Reagan and Fidel Castro are related.

For more than ten years during his youth, Tom Jefferson practiced playing the violin three hours a day.

H. L. Mencken once described Herbert Hoover as a "a fat Coolidge." Hoover, in turn, referred to Franklin D. Roosevelt as "a chameleon on plaid."

A dozen U.S. Presidents were related to kings. Richard Nixon is a descendant of King Leka I of Albania. He too was exiled.

George Washington once said, "Candor is not a more conspicuous trait in the character of Government, than it is of individuals."

Thirteen times a man has been elected President without winning a majority of the popular vote.

Said Dwight Eisenhower, "I make it a practice to avoid hating anyone."

Water was taken from the Jordan River to the White House for the baptism of Benjamin Harrison's granddaughter.

John Adams was somewhat distressed because no member of his family attended his inauguration.

In the *Whig Circular* of March 4, 1843, Abraham Lincoln was quoted as a saying, "An individual undertakes to live by borrowing, soon finds his original means devoured by interest, and next, no one to borrow from; so must it be with the government."

Jimmy Carter was the only full-term President not to nominate a single U.S. Supreme Court Justice. FDR nominated nine.

Said Thomas Jefferson, "I cannot live without books."

John Tyler, our tenth President, was Harry Truman's great uncle.

Theodore Roosevelt said, "Every man owes some of his time to the upbuilding of the profession to which he belongs."

Upon leaving the White House, Andrew Jackson had only two regrets. He had not been able to hang John C. Calhoun or shoot Henry Clay!

On the subject of chance, James A. Garfield once remarked, "Luck is ignisfatuus. You may follow it to ruin but never to victory."

After his failure to gain a second term in 1840, President Martin Van Buren had this to say about his defeat to Whig candidate William Henry Harrison: "We were sung down, drunk down, and lied down."

During one Thanksgiving during the Carter administration, a wild turkey was loose for two days on the White House grounds.

Many pro-abortionists and feminists battled Ronald Reagan because of his view against abortion. In 1986, Reagan remarked, "I don't think that I'm trying to do something that is taking a privilege away from womanhood, because I don't think womanhood should be considering murder a privilege."

When George Washington died in December of 1799, he owned 277 slaves, all of whom were eventually freed.

FDR once used this parable in discussing problem solving: "The Chinese have a story based on three or four thousand years of civilization. Two Chinese coolies were arguing heatedly in the midst of a crowd. A stranger expressed surprise that no blows were being struck. His Chinese friend replied, 'The man who strikes first admits that his ideas have given out.' "

William McKinley's mother, upon learning of her son's election as the 25th President, was heard to remark, "Oh God, keep him humble." She had little to fear, for her son remained so.

Abraham Lincoln received the first dispatch by air. During the Civil War, balloonist Thaddeus Lowe relayed a military report on Confederate positions.

In reflecting upon the Presidency, John Quincy Adams stated, "I can scarcely conceive a more harassing, wearying, teasing condition of existence."

James K. Polk's last words were whispered to his wife: "I love you, Sarah, I love you."

Theodore Roosevelt once said, "In the White House you do not live. You are just Exhibit A."

During Richard Nixon's term, the White House staff increased from 220 to 510 people.

It was Lincoln who said, "Any man over 40 is responsible for the engraving on his own face."

Andrew Johnson, our 17th President, was named after Andrew Jackson. At the time of Johnson's birth, Andrew Jackson wasn't even President, but a well-known attorney in Tennessee.

Theodore Roosevelt believed in hard work. He once said, "Never throughout history has a man who lived a life of ease left a name worth remembering."

Two Presidents are buried side-by-side: the Adamses.

"Great lives never go out; they *go on*." So said Benjamin Harrison.

Both John Tyler, Sr. and his son, John Tyler, Jr. (the tenth U.S. President) were governors of Virginia.

Franklin D. Roosevelt once advised, "When you come to the end of your rope, tie a knot and hang on."

Actress Jane Wyman, Ronald Reagan's first wife, was referred to as "Button-nose" by her actor-husband.

George Washington observed, "Few men have virtue to withstand the highest bidder."

In August of 1982 Ronald Reagan strolled into the Rose Garden with Liberian President Samuel K. Doe and introduced him to the media as "Chairman Moe."

All of us may benefit from Abraham Lincoln's words of wisdom: "Better to remain silent and be thought a fool than to speak and remove all doubt."

Two Presidents have written books which became television series: *Crusade in Europe* by Dwight Eisenhower and *Profiles in Courage* by John F. Kennedy.

Theodore Roosevelt voiced, "I despise a man who surrenders his conscience to a multitude as much as I do one who surrenders it to one man."

John Quincy Adams was accused of being exorbitant and spendthrifty when he used public dollars to purchase a chess set and a billiard table for the White House.

Twenty-seven counties have been named for Vice Presidents.

Thomas Jefferson has told us, "I never considered a difference of opinion in politics, in religion, in philosophy, as a cause for withdrawing from a friend."

Millard Fillmore was the last Whig Party President.

Abraham Lincoln's small yellow mixed-breed dog was named Jip.

William McKinley possessed a rare and remarkable talent for remembering names and faces, often astonishing those he met a second time.

"Organization cannot make a genius out of an incompetent." The man who said that ought to know — his name was Dwight D. Eisenhower.

Herbert Hoover and Richard Nixon were distant cousins.

The first U.S. ballistic missile submarine was named in honor of a President. You guessed it — *The George Washington.*

Thomas Jefferson said, "It is a part of the American character to consider nothing as desperate; to surmount every difficulty by resolution and contrivance."

During Lyndon Johnson's term in office, an enterprising Texan sold small jars of water from the Pedernales River, which flows past the Johnson Ranch.

Said Woodrow Wilson, "If you think too much about being reelected, it is very difficult to be worth reelecting."

Theodore Roosevelt was superstitious, and his belief in charms and omens led him to carry a rabbit's foot throughout the Spanish-American War.

Abraham Lincoln once walked 34 miles in one day while on an errand.

In his 1929 inaugural address Herbert Hoover mistakenly announced, "In no nations are the fruits of accomplishment more secure." The Great Depression was just around the corner.

In 1884 showman P.T. Barnum offered ex-President Grant $100,000 to let him exhibit Civil War trophies which Grant was sending to the Smithsonian Institution. Grant found the suggestion repugnant and refused to make himself one of Barnum's circus attractions, even though he was in desperate financial need.

In his Farm Book, Thomas Jefferson recorded he had 204 slaves.

The first night game in major league baseball was played on May 24, 1935 at Cincinnati. FDR pushed a remote control switch at the White House and lit Crosley Field.

Trying to remain calm after repeated German submarine attacks on American shipping, Woodrow Wilson told author Ida Tarbell, "My great duty is not to see red." But Germany forced Wilson's hand, and in 1917, he asked Congress for a declaration of war.

Lincoln once said, "It is as a peacemaker that the lawyer has a superior opportunity."

Perhaps more than any other American, John Adams prevented our young republic from going bankrupt. In serving as an overseas ambassador, he obtained four loans from Holland, the last coming in 1788.

The "Bound Boy of Raleigh" was a nickname pinned on Andrew Johnson, referring to his days as an indentured servant.

James A. Garfield once commented, "I am conscious of not being fit for the partisan work of politics, although I believe in partisanship within reasonable limits."

Ex-President Rutherford B. Hayes spent many happy years reflecting upon his life during his retirement at Spiegel Grove in Fremont, Ohio. Reflecting at his estate was easy — "Spiegel" is the German word for "mirror."

Theodore Roosevelt wrote a total of 37 books.

Abraham Lincoln said the definition of democracy was quite simple: "As ~uld not be a slave, so I would not be a slave master."

~ht Eisenhower's family originally came from Germany. Spelled " the name has been translated as meaning "iron striker" or ~t."

In a letter written to George Washington in 1792, Thomas Jefferson offered this advice: "Delay is preferable to error."

Following the 1880 Republican Convention, a couple of delegates found the dazed nominee, James A. Garfield, in his Chicago hotel room thinking aloud, "I don't know whether I am glad or not."

What was U.S. Grant's weapon he carried in battle during the last part of the Civil War? It was neither a sword nor a pistol. Grant had only a jackknife, which he used to whittle twigs while battles raged.

New York boss Roscoe Conkling saw Theodore Roosevelt only as "a dentifical young man with more teeth than brains."

Dwight D. Eisenhower left this bit of advice to national leaders: "Get all the good facts and all the good counsel you can and then do what's best for America."

Learning of his nomination for President in 1928, Herbert Hoover declared, "My country owes me nothing. It gave me, as it gives every boy and girl, a chance . . . I am indebted to my country far beyond any power to repay."

Some political experts feel a Vice-Presidential candidate does not really help a Presidential candidate. The trick is to find a running mate who won't hurt the top candidate. In 1968, Richard Nixon told advisors prior to selecting Spiro Agnew that he wished he could run alone.

Concerning the Vice Presidency, John Adams wrote his wife, "My country has in its wisdom contrived for me the most insignificant office that ever the invention of man contrived, or his imagination conceived." He added further, "I am Vice President. In this I am nothing."

President Reagan had a motto on his desk which read: "There is no limit to what a man can do if he doesn't care who gets the credit."

Thomas Jefferson observed, "A mind always well employed is always content."

A close friend of President Chester Arthur was tobacco king, R.G. Dun, who kept his companion well-supplied with cigars.

Not until 1864 did the Union armies consistently defeat the South in battle. Prior to his second election, a war-weary, exhausted Lincoln said, "I am a slow walker, but I never walk back."

The 42nd President was christened with *two* middle names: George Herbert Walker Bush.

Ex-President Jimmy Carter had this to say about the outspoken Jerry Falwell in 1986: "In a very Christian way, as far as I'm concerned, he can go to hell."

When Lafayette visited John Quincy Adams in 1826, he brought an alligator with him to the White House. The Frenchman had received it as a gift enroute to Washington. The reptile was kept in the East Room.

Prior to his service in the American Revolution, George Washington served as Justice of the Peace in Fairfax County, Virginia.

Few historians note (or really care) that Millard Fillmore was married twice. His first wife died in 1853 shortly after he left office. Five years later he married Caroline McIntosh, the "apple" of his eye.

Only two people besides President Wilson could decode secret messages from Europe during World War I. Colonel House and Edith Wilson also knew the code. Not even the Secretary of State or members of the War Department were privileged to such information.

In 1809 at the end of Jefferson's second term, there were 27 daily newspapers in the U.S. No doubt this was still too many for some politicians.

At the 1908 Republican convention, Senator Henry Cabot Lodge paid tribute to out-going President Theodore Roosevelt. His remarks set off a cheering, foot-stomping demonstration which lasted a full forty-nine minutes.

As George Washington lay dying, he asked his aide, Tobias Lear, not to bury his body for two days after death. Washington feared he might awaken inside his coffin.

Said Calvin Coolidge, "I do not believe the government should seek social legislation in the guise of taxation. If we are to adopt socialism it should be presented to the people as socialism and not under the guise of a law to collect revenue."

While serving as Vice President, John Adams's salary was only one fifth that of the President's. Adams found his $5,000 yearly income quite insufficient. And by the time he became Chief Executive, Adams suffered from palsy and had lost all his teeth.

President Franklin Roosevelt was a real admirer of the young Texas Congressman, Lyndon Johnson. FDR once told friends about Johnson, "That's the kind of man I could have been if I hadn't had a Harvard education."

Lincoln once said of a fellow lawyer, "He can compress the most words into the smallest ideas of any man I ever met."

James Garfield was once quoted, "Territory is but the body of a nation. The people who inhabit its hills and valleys are its soul, its spirit, its life."

In 1787, Thomas Jefferson wrote to Maria Cosway, "I am born to lose everything I love."

After observing the nudes and other works of art at the New York City Modern Art Show in 1913, Theodore Roosevelt referred to the exhibit as "cave man art."

Lincoln's attitude toward the conquered rebel states, and his philosophy of reconstruction, was summed up in one brief comment to Sherman and Grant in 1865: "Let 'em up easy."

Harry Truman bore none of the animosity FDR held towards Herbert Hoover. Said Truman, "I hold Mr. Hoover in very high regard. I think he is a great American and will someday be so recognized even by the people who have defamed him." History has proven Truman correct.

The first Presidential staff to use typewriters was that of James Garfield's in 1881.

While vacationing at Yellowstone National Park in 1907, Taft told his wife and son, Charlie, "Politics make me sick."

The first President to employ ghost writers was FDR. Though past Chief Executives had assistance in their speeches by various aides and friends, Roosevelt depended on ghost writers for many of his orations.

William McKinley reminded his countrymen, "Unlike any other nation, here the people rule. Their law is supreme."

Traditionally, a President selects three portraits of former Presidents to hang in the Cabinet Room of the White House. Nixon had chosen Lincoln, Wilson and Eisenhower. Gerald Ford replaced Wilson's portrait with that of Truman's.

On the eve of signing a trade embargo against Cuba, John Kennedy ordered Pierre Salinger to buy and stockpile 1500 Havana cigars.

When James A. Garfield was a child, he watched members of a local church being baptized in a small pond and listened while the preacher talked about cleansing the people of their sins. Later in the summer, when the pond was covered with a green scum, Garfield said he knew what the green stuff was. It was the sins rising to the surface.

One of the reasons William Henry Harrison actively campaigned was to counteract the Democratic charges that he was "an old, broken-down, feeble man."

Lyndon B. Johnson was the first Democratic President to carry the state of Vermont.

In his last address to Congress, George Washington stated, "Knowledge is in every country the surest basis of public happiness."

Richard Nixon's daughter, Julie, married David Eisenhower, grandson of the 34th President. This led to Nixon to introduce himself as "President Eisenhower's grandson's father-in-law, Dick Nixon."

When Franklin Pierce was elected to the U.S. Senate in 1836, he was its youngest member. When he was elected President, he was the youngest man ever elected to that office at the time.

An old friend called ex-President Harry Truman in Independence, Missouri. "What are you doing?" he inquired. "I'm doing as I damn please — when the Madam will let me," shouted Truman over the telephone.

Lyndon Johnson once requested one of his speech writers to "give me some jokes for my statement on behalf of retarded children."

Reagan once commented about television reporters, "I understand ABC's been having some budget problems. The news division's already laid off three hair stylists."

John Kennedy often cited Oscar Wilde's observation of the power of the press: "In America the President reigns for four years, but Journalism governs forever."

The first incumbent President to visit Holland was George Bush. His trip took place in mid-July of 1989.

Herbert Hoover failed only one subject in college — German.

Thomas Jefferson contended he learned to speak Spanish after just 19 days at sea. When John Quincy Adams heard this, he remarked, "But Mr. Jefferson tells large stories."

Jimmy Carter once quipped, "Show me a good loser and I will show you a loser."

During the 1988 campaign George Bush reminded a crowd, "I believe that America does have a special mission in this world; we are the flagship of freedom."

In 1832 Dr. Thomas Harris extracted a bullet from President Andrew Jackson's arm. It had been there for 26 years following a duel.

In My Opinion

The Ten Most Physically Fit Presidents While In Office
(Based on overall health and any athletic ability)

1. Theodore Roosevelt

2. Gerald Ford

3. James A. Garfield

4. Harry S Truman

5. Ronald Reagan

6. George Bush

7. Jimmy Carter

8. James Madison

9. Thomas Jefferson

10. Herbert Hoover and George Washington

The Ten Most Physically Unfit Presidents

1. James K. Polk

2. William Henry Harrison

3. Zachary Taylor

4. Warren G. Harding

5. Chester Arthur

6. Ulysses S. Grant

7. Lyndon Johnson

8. Franklin D. Roosevelt

9. Richard Nixon

10. Woodrow Wilson and Abraham Lincoln

The Ten Handsomest Presidents

1. John F. Kennedy

2. Franklin Pierce

3. Warren G. Harding

4. Dwight D. Eisenhower

5. James A. Garfield

6. George Bush

7. James Monroe

8. Gerald Ford

9. Jimmy Carter

10. Thomas Jefferson and Grover Cleveland

The Ten Best Looking Wives of Presidents

1. Ellen Herndon Arthur (died before entering the White House)

2. Jacqueline Kennedy

3. Frances Folsom Cleveland (married at the White House)

4. Rachel Jackson (died prior to Andrew's first term)

5. Rosalynn Carter

6. Betty Ford

7. Lucretia Garfield

8. Grace Coolidge

9. Nancy Reagan

10. Lady Bird Johnson and Sarah Childress Polk

The Ten Most Outgoing or Extroverted Presidents

1. Theodore Roosevelt

2. John F. Kennedy

3. Franklin D. Roosevelt

4. Harry S Truman

5. Dwight D. Eisenhower

6. William Howard Taft

7. George Bush

8. Martin Van Buren

9. William McKinley

10. Ronald Reagan and Lyndon Johnson

The Ten Most Introverted Presidents

1. Richard Nixon

2. Franklin Pierce

3. Calvin Coolidge

4. James K. Polk

5. Chester Arthur

6. Millard Fillmore

7. Herbert Hoover

8. Andrew Johnson

9. George Washington

10. Woodrow Wilson

The Ten Wealthiest Men Upon Becoming President

1. Herbert Hoover

2. John F. Kennedy

3. Franklin D. Roosevelt

4. Theodore Roosevelt

5. George Washington

6. George Bush

7. John Quincy Adams

8. Lyndon Johnson

9. Benjamin Harrison

10. Warren G. Harding and William Howard Taft

Answers To Quiz Time

1. Abe Lincoln. Vice President Andrew Johnson showed up drunk for his oath and made some rude remarks inside the Capitol on March 4, 1865. Johnson's reputation was never the same after that day, and he was virtually powerless when he assumed the Presidency following Lincoln's death a month later.

2. William Howard Taft, who was appointed to that post by Teddy Roosevelt in 1906. Taft was also governor of the Philippines.

3. Ronald Reagan. The 73-year-old President took just 30 seconds to defeat Dan Lurie of Wantagh, New York. An official White House photo recorded the event, which took place inside the Oval Office. Said Lurie, "I wasn't ready for him to be so strong." The bout took place on February 16, 1984.

4. The President wanted a new porch, so the South Portico was added on to the White House. The artwork on the back of the bill had to be changed.

5. Millard Fillmore. The photo was taken in 1980.

6. Dwight D. Eisenhower. Eisenhower also injured his leg in a game against Tufts University.

7. William Henry Harrison in 1841.

8. Warren G. Harding. Thomas was a newsboy for Harding's newspaper, the *Marion Star*.

9. Zachary Taylor.

10. Richard Nixon, during the Watergate scandals and prior to firing his two top aides. The remark was made to Leonard Garment.

11. Theodore Roosevelt. An insatiable reader and writer, Teddy could read a page in the time a normal person reads a sentence. John F. Kennedy was also a speed reader.

12. John Quincy Adams.

13. Andrew Jackson.

14. Lyndon Johnson.

15. Harry Truman. George Bush also did this, installing a horseshoe pit in the spring of 1989.

16. Abraham Lincoln. Abe was on his way home near Spencerville, Indiana after borrowing a book from a neighbor.

17. FDR, who sailed the boat during summers at Campobello.

18. Martin Van Buren in the 1840 election when he lost to William Henry Harrison.

19. Woodrow Wilson in 1918. Four years later, there were efforts to nominate Henry Ford for President, but this failed also.

20. Ronald Reagan, former president of the Screen Actors Guild.

21. George Washington.

22. Thomas Edison. The Ohio inventor often worked 20-hour days, while Coolidge worked about six hours and took plenty of vacations.

23. Herbert Hoover, a Quaker. His wife, Lou Henry, was an Episcopalian and a teacher in Monterey, California. There was no Protestant minister in the town so Father Ramon Mestres, a family friend and justice of the peace, married the couple.

24. Gerald Ford, who was originally named Leslie (after his biological father Leslie King), and later Gerald (after his adopted father).

25. North Dakota.

26. Jimmy Carter.

27. Dwight Eisenhower, while at Columbia University from 1948-1952.

28. James Monroe in 1831.

29. William McKinley. At the age of nine, McKinley moved to Poland, *Ohio*, a small village in Mahoning County! He attended the academy there and later went to Allegheny College in Meadville, Pennsylvania.

30. 14.

31. Andrew Jackson of Tennessee.

32. Ronald Reagan.

33. Harry Truman. President John Kennedy later changed its design and renamed it the Presidential Medal of Freedom. Past recipients have included Bob Hope, John Ford, Kirk Douglas, and many others.

34. John Quincy Adams and Theodore Roosevelt (second wife).

35. Chester Arthur.

36. William Henry Harrison, who gained fame as a military leader and office holder of several state and national positions. In 1834, he was appointed clerk of the Hamilton County Common Pleas Court in Ohio.

37. None. The U.S. asked for and got nothing from the defeated countries.

38. U.S. Grant in 1872 when he defeated, among others, Charles O'Conor (a Catholic Presidential contender), Victoria Woodhull, and Negro Frederick Douglass.

39. FDR. His wife often carried a loaded pistol in her purse.

40. Calvin Coolidge.

41. Gerald Ford, who in 1976 debated Jimmy Carter. Carter won the debates and the Presidency.

42. Andrew Johnson. This was on July 26, 1866, when David Farragut was rewarded by Congress with this title. Top ranking naval officers prior to this were called commodores.

43. Ronald Reagan, on November 6, 1984.

44. Abraham Lincoln.

45. Thomas Jefferson, when his grandson, James Madison Randolph, was born there on January 17, 1806.

46. "The First Gentleman."

47. Campobello, the summer home of Franklin Delano Roosevelt, which is located in New Brunswick Province, Canada.

48. John Quincy Adams and his mother, Abigail.

49. John Tyler. Judge Tyler and Jefferson attended the College of William and Mary together.

50. Chicago, with nearly 40.

51. Dwight Eisenhower. In the early 1920's, "Ike" was assigned by the army to Panama. A bat got into his bedroom, and the future President killed it. This was an illegal act, because bats ate disease-carrying mosquitoes, and the Panamanian government protected them.

52. James Madison in 1812. Upper Canada and the St. Lawrence Valley were British strongholds.

53. 7.

54. "Bloviate," which means, according to Webster's *Third International Dictionary*, "to talk or speak verbosely or windily."

55. Woodrow Wilson. While attending Princeton, he was the team's assistant manager.

56. The actor was introduced five times by host Garry Moore. Every time one of the guest panelists said "Ah" or made a mistake in their questioning, Reagan went backstage to be reintroduced. His "secret" was that he wanted the questioning done like a movie take, with no mistakes. On a later TV show, "What's My Line," he was the mystery guest and fooled the panelists by stuttering and changing his voice.

57. FDR.

58. Grover Cleveland. In 1897, the out-going President witnessed the swearing-in of William McKinley, even though his foot was badly swollen from gout.

59. James A. Garfield, who, at the age of 15, worked on the canals in Ohio.

60. George Bush.

61. Fishing.

62. Richard Nixon. In July of 1969, he spoke with the astronauts 238,000 miles away during their journey to the moon.

63. George Washington, to Jean Pierre Blanchard of France. Blanchard carried the letter with him on a hot-air balloon flight from Philadelphia to New Jersey.

127

64. John F. Kennedy. His grandmother was 96 years old. Her husband, John "Honey Fitz" Fitzgerald had been mayor of Boston at one time.

65. It is the black bag which contains top-secret military and communication codes that follow the President wherever he goes, to be used in the event of a national crisis.

66. Martin Van Buren by the Democrats in the First Presbyterian Church in Baltimore, Maryland, and William Henry Harrison at the First Lutheran (Zion) Church by the Whig Party. This church is also in Baltimore.

67. Teddy Roosevelt.

68. James Monroe in 1820.

69. Dwight Eisenhower, a football player at West Point.

70. Warren G. Harding on March 14, 1923.

71. Why, Woodrow Wilson, of course.

72. Harry Truman. The numbers represented May 7, 1945, the date Germany surrendered to the U.S., ending the war in Europe.

73. None other than Franklin Pierce. Though this was his given name, it does not appear on any public record.

74. William and Mary.

75. Calvin Coolidge in 1923, following Warren Harding's death.

76. Richard Nixon, while vacationing at Camp David in 1972.

77. Ronald Reagan, on February 5, 1985, the same date he delivered his State of the Union address. Reagan was 74 years old.

78. Jimmy Carter.

79. Theodore Roosevelt, in the interests of conservation.

80. John Quincy Adams. After Stuart began the painting, he became ill and died. Thomas Sully completed the portrait of our sixth President.

81. Herbert Hoover, who selected Charles Francis Adams III to run the Navy. Adams was also the great-great grandson of our second President, John Adams.

82. Andrew Jackson.

83. Gerald Ford.

84. Rutherford B. Hayes. Thomas Edison recorded his voice at the White House in the 1870's. This recording is lost, but most of the other Presidents after Hayes have had their voices recorded. I have heard the actual voices of Grover Cleveland, William McKinley, Theodore Roosevelt, and Woodrow Wilson.

85. Abraham Lincoln.

86. Franklin D. Roosevelt.

87. Thomas Jefferson, with more than 1,230, extending to eleven generations.

88. James K. Polk and his "veep" George Dallas on May 1, 1847.

89. Jean Kirkpatrick. As U.N. Ambassador during the first half of the 1980's, she was also the first female member of Reagan's cabinet.

90. Martin Van Buren.

91. Teddy Roosevelt, who was once Assistant Secretary of the Navy. The date is May 5.

92. John Adams, when Thomas Jefferson was sworn in. Adams's son, John Quincy, also refused to attend his successor's swearing-in ceremonies, those of Andrew Jackson's.

93. The Eisenhowers.

94. The House brings forth the charges, the Senate acts as the jury, and the Chief Justice is the judge.

95. Zachary Taylor, when he died in office in 1850.

96. Harry Truman. The reason for this was Truman's blue Army uniform. His grandmother, a Southern sympathizer who vividly remembered the Civil War, ordered him to leave. Truman may have been an outstanding and

gallant artillery officer in World War I, but this didn't impress his grand-mother.

97. James Garfield, William McKinley, and Warren Harding of Ohio.

98. Jimmy and Rosalynn Carter.

99. James Buchanan, who graduated first in his class in 1809.

100. Franklin D. Roosevelt.

101. Woodrow Wilson, while stumping the country trying to convince the people that the U.S. should join the League of Nations.

102. Warren G. Harding. Amos Kling, his father-in-law, didn't visit the Harding home until 22 years after the wedding.

103. Martin Van Buren.

104. Dwight Eisenhower, whose grandson, David, worked for a Philadelphia daily paper. You might have heard of David's father-in-law, also a baseball lover — Richard Nixon.

105. Franklin Pierce.

106. Abraham Lincoln, who spoke before Mathew Brady's raised cameras in 1861.

107. Zachary Taylor on March 5, 1849.

108. *Marine One.*

109. Woodrow Wilson, when it was rumored that he died on February 2, 1924. But Wilson clung to life and died at 11:15 A.M. the next day.

110. Jimmy Carter. He was not reelected.

111. This was James K. Polk, then Speaker of the House. Polk, a southern slave owner, defeated Clay in the 1844 Presidential election.

112. *Starfish.* It was also in this film he met his future wife, actress Nancy Davis.

113. James Monroe in 1820. The lone dissenter cast his ballot for John Quincy Adams, believing that no one but George Washington should be accorded

this high distinction.

114. FDR, when he visited with Churchill at Casablanca in January of 1943.

115. William Henry Harrison, born on February 9, 1773.

116. Herbert Hoover in 1929, at a banquet in Edison's honor.

117. Warren G. Harding.

118. William McKinley, during his first term.

119. Harry Truman, whose father, John Anderson Truman, stood at 5'4" and weighed 140 pounds. Papa Truman, however, had a reputation as a tough guy who could defend himself quite adequately.

120. Zachary Taylor in 1849.

121. James A. Garfield and Chester Arthur.

122. William Howard Taft, and he was right. In the 1912 Presidential election, he finished third behind Woodrow Wilson and Theodore Roosevelt.

123. John Quincy Adams.

124. Ronald Reagan, said to him by friends while making movies for Warner Brothers in the late 1940's.

125. Franklin D. Roosevelt.

126. Harry Truman, whose daughter Margaret christened the ship. It was named after Truman's home state.

127. Just one — Washington. Four state capitals are named in honor of Presidents.

128. Dwight Eisenhower.

129. Zachary Taylor.

130. Either Theodore Roosevelt or Woodrow Wilson.

131. Yes. In April of 1860, the Democrats met for ten days in Charleston, South Carolina without deciding upon a candidate. Two months later, the Democrats met in Baltimore to select Stephen Douglas, who was defeated by Lincoln.

132. Thomas Jefferson.

133. Richard Nixon, while attending law school at Duke University.

134. William Henry Harrison. In November of 1811, 700 Wyandots, Shawnees, Potawatomies, and Miamis led by The Prophet attacked Harrison's camp in Indiana. The sun had just come up, and Harrison was putting on his boots as gunfire echoed throughout the camp. He ordered a servant to fetch his gray steed, but in the confusion of battle, Harrison had to borrow an officer's black horse. The Indians were under orders to kill Harrison and killed the officer riding the gray mare. "Old Tippecanoe" had luck on his side that day.

135. Warren G. Harding, a graduate of Ohio Central College (Iberia).

136. William Harrison Dempsey, better known as "Jack" Dempsey.

137. Rutherford B. Hayes, who nearly died from Confederate bullets and had three horses shot from under him. He served in the Union Army during the four years fighting between the North and South.

138. Herbert Hoover, born in Iowa on August 10, 1874.

139. John Tyler.

140. Benjamin Harrison as a student at Miami University in Oxford, Ohio.

141. Martin Van Buren.

142. Abraham Lincoln. The 1909 penny celebrated the 100th anniversary of Abe's birth.

143. Andrew Johnson, who was four years old when his father perished.

144. George Bush.

145. U.S. Grant, while serving under the command of Zachary Taylor during the Mexican War. The play took place in Corpus Christi, Texas. Taylor, incidentally, became the 12th President.

146. Millard Fillmore, our 13th Chief Executive. His heroic efforts, however, did little to boost his popularity among Americans. Fillmore signed the Fugitive Slave Act into law and this, along with his compromising nature, projected an image of weakness to both northerners and southerners.

147. Harry Truman, who welcomed India's Shrimati Pandit on May 12, 1952.

148. Roger B. Taney, who administered the oath of office to Van Buren, Harrison, Polk, Taylor, Pierce, Buchanan, and Lincoln.

149. James Madison.

150. James K. Polk in 1844 or Warren G. Harding in 1920.

151. Eisenhower, during his first term.

152. Lyndon Johnson, who was not much of a sports enthusiast.

153. They were both Adamses, John and his son, John Quincy.

154. All close friends of the President are given a series of numbers to put on the outside of the envelope. This code changes with each Chief Executive. Jimmy Carter, for instance, used an old phone number of Rosalynn's; Ronald Reagan's code was a number with special meaning to him and his wife.

155. Abe Lincoln, whose son, Robert, went on to serve his nation in a number of capacities.

156. Ronald Reagan.

157. FDR, whose Scottish terrier, Fala, received its stripe during World War II. Soon, hundreds of thousands of dog owners sent one dollar to the President to have their canines commissioned. The money was spent towards the war effort.

158. George Washington, who appointed ten of them.

159. James Monroe.

160. Gerald Ford. Instead, he took a job at Yale coaching football and boxing, earning $2,400 per year which helped him attend law school there.

161. Dwight D. Eisenhower. In 1958, "Ike" made history with a taped Christmas greeting to the people on earth, sent by satellite.

162. Martin Van Buren.

163. John F. Kennedy.

164. Jefferson, Grant, and Wilson.

165. Frank Pierce, who attended Bowdoin College in Brunswick, Maine.

166. Jimmy Carter.

167. James Monroe.

168. Zachary Taylor. Though a Southerner and a slave holder, Taylor was a staunch Unionist and threatened to hang Dixie leaders who wanted to set up a confederacy.

169. Richard Nixon, when he ran for governor of California in 1962. He lost.

170. Woodrow Wilson, whose daughter, Nellie, married William G. McAdoo while he served in the Wilson cabinet.

171. James Madison.

172. Ronald Reagan on January 19, 1985, at the end of his first term.

173. Television.

174. Ulysses S. Grant.

175. Herbert Hoover at Stanford. He briefly played football, then became the team's equipment manager.

176. Amy Carter. Papa Jimmy, a talented carpenter and woodworker, was bombarded with requests for "Amy Carter Tree Houses."

177. Warren G. Harding.

178. Teddy Roosevelt. The palindrome is A MAN A PLAN A CANAL PANAMA. Roosevelt supposedly said of the canal acquisition, "We stole it from them fair and square."

179. Dwight Eisenhower, who was so described in the 1915 edition of the *West Point Howitzer*.

180. Andrew Jackson, who defeated the British-controlled Creek Indians in Mississippi. This was in 1813, and Jackson's harsh peace terms netted 23,000,000 acres of land from warring tribes.

181. Ronald Reagan in 1981. He stipulated, among other things, that gray-striped trousers be worn.

182. Thomas Jefferson; the man in the dual role was John Marshall.

183. These accusations were leveled by incumbent William Howard Taft against former President Teddy Roosevelt when T.R. ran on the Progressive (Bull Moose) ticket in 1912. With the Republican Party split, the Democrat Woodrow Wilson won easily.

184. Abraham Lincoln. Thursday, August 6, 1863 was set as the day, mainly because of Union victories at Vicksburg and Gettysburg. Later, the day of Thanksgiving was changed to November, following the traditional harvest celebration in conjunction with the early Pilgrims in 1621.

185. Richard Nixon.

186. FDR, beginning his fourth term. The 32nd President was in poor health, and also thought it improper to have festivities while Americans were dying on battlefields during World War II.

187. John F. Kennedy, for a brief time in 1945. This news agency was owned by William Randolph Hearst, a friend of Kennedy's father.

188. Benjamin Harrison.

189. William Howard Taft, when he was Governor-General of the Philippines in 1901.

190. FDR.

191. Jonathan Chapman, better known as "Johnny Appleseed."

192. "The Michigan Fight Song."

193. William McKinley. "Rainbow City" was the name of the Pan American Exposition in Buffalo, New York.

194. The Russian dictator, Joseph Stalin. This took place in late November of 1943 when Roosevelt, Churchill, and Stalin met in Tehran.

195. It took him 13 days in a bouncing carriage over rough roads.

196. George Bush, the Vice President at the time.

197. William Howard Taft, while governor of the Philippines in 1901.

198. John F. Kennedy, whose young son, John-John, also called him "Naughty Daddy" when the two were playing.

199. Franklin D. Roosevelt. Sandburg made his remarks during a radio broadcast in November of 1940.

200. John Quincy Adams.

Answers To Matching

Nicknames: A - 6; B - 1; C - 3; D - 5; E - 4; F - 7; and G - 2.

Yachts: A - 2; B - 4; C - 3; and D - 1.

Last Words: A - 3; B - 5; C - 2; D - 4; E - 1; and F - 6.

More Nicknames: A - 4; B - 5; C - 6; D - 3; E - 1; F - 2; and G - 7.

Presidential Portraits: A - 3; B - 5; C - 1; D - 4; and E - 2.

Answers To Presidents' Wives
And First Ladies Only

1. William Henry Harrison. His wife, Anna, was granted $25,000 by Congress and the bill was signed by our tenth President, John Tyler.

2. Rosalynn Carter.

3. Mary Todd Lincoln, after her son's death; Willie died in 1862.

4. Dolley Madison in 1844. When inventor Samuel Morse handed her the first message "What Hath God Wrought?", she was asked to reply while standing at the telegraph in Washington, D.C.

5. Eliza McCardle Johnson, wife of the seventeenth President. She was 16 years old.

6. Jane Pierce. Nicknamed the "Shadow in the White House," she mourned the death of her son, Benny, prior to her husband's term as the fourteenth President. Two other sons died in infancy, and Mrs. Pierce felt a curse had fallen on her and the President.

7. Eleanor Roosevelt.

8. Jackie Kennedy. In the 1970's during her marriage to multimillionaire Aristotle Onassis, Jackie was photographed "in the buff" by a paparazzo who cruised offshore Scorpios, her island retreat in the Mediterranean, and took the picture with a telescopic lens from a mile away. Thousands of photographs were distributed and sold throughout the world. Among the U.S. publications publishing photos was *Hustler* magazine.

9. Lou Henry Hoover, who was a freshman at Stanford when she met Herbert.

10. Mrs. Benjamin Harrison in 1889.

11. Frances Cleveland, who "tied the knot" less than five years after her husband's death.

12. Elizabeth Monroe. In 1830, she had a seizure and fell into some burning logs in her fireplace.

13. Anna Harrison, who was ill when her husband took the oath of office. She stayed in Cincinnati, Ohio.

14. Rosalynn Carter.

15. Mary Lincoln, whose cousin, William Todd, created a sketch at the suggestion of fellow settlers.

16. Mrs. Florence Harding, wife of the twenty-ninth President.

17. Martha Washington.

18. Anna Harrison, who was safely transported from New Jersey to New York. Due to her husband's term in office of only one month, she never served in the White House as First Lady.

19. Her husband, the President. Eisenhower was an accomplished landscape artist.

20. Louisa Johnson Adams, wife of John Quincy Adams.

21. Sarah Polk, who also disapproved of alcoholic beverages and dancing.

22. Mrs. Benjamin Harrison.

23. Dolley Madison, in writing to her sister in 1814. Her husband-President was forced to leave the capital to join American forces when British troops marched toward Washington, D.C. Tricky, eh?

24. Mary Lincoln's. This happened in the late summer of 1863 just a few weeks after she was involved in a serious carriage accident, which hospitalized her. The injured youth, incidentally, suffered a broken leg, and Mrs. Lincoln showered the boy and his family with food, flowers, and gifts.

25. Anna Symmes Harrison, wife of our ninth President.

26. Lou Henry Hoover. All were provided a fine meal.

27. Jacqueline Bouvier Kennedy, who began horse-riding competition at age 6.

28. Ellen Axson Wilson. Her father was a Presbyterian minister in Rome, *Georgia*!

29. Thelma Ryan "Pat" Nixon. She also had bit parts as a dancer in films.

30. Lady Bird Johnson. LBJ later bought her an elegant diamond ring.

Bibliography

Albertazzie, Col. Ralph and ter Horst, Jerry F. *The Flying Whitehouse*, Coward, McCann and Geoghegan, Inc., New York, 1979.

Ambrose, Stephen F. *Ike: Abilene to Berlin*, Harper and Row, New York, 1973.

Andrist, Ralph K. *George Washington: A Biography in His Own Words*, Volumes I and II, Newsweek, Inc., New York, 1972.

Belden, Henry S., III. *Grand Tour of Ida Saxton McKinley and Sister Mary Saxton Barber - 1869*, The Reserve Printing Company, Canton, Ohio, 1985.

Brodie, Fawn M. *Thomas Jefferson - An Intimate History*, W.W. Norton and Co., New York, 1974.

Burner, David. *Herbert Hoover; A Public Life*, Knopf, New York, 1979.

Caroli, Betty Boyd. *First Ladies*, Oxford University Press, New York, 1987.

Chase, Harold W. and Leman, Allen H. *Kennedy and the Press*, Thomas Y. Crowell Company, New York, 1965.

Corwin, Norman. *Trivializing America*, Lyle Stuart, Inc., Secaucus, New Jersey, 1983.

Criss, Mildred. *Jefferson's Daughter*, Dodd, Mead, and Co., New York, 1948.

DeGregorio, William. *The Complete Book of U.S. Presidents*, Dembner Books, New York, 1984.

Ferrell, Robert H. *Truman - A Centenary Remembrance*, Viking Press, New York, 1984.

Filler, Louis, ed. *The President Speaks: From William McKinley to Lyndon Johnson*, G.P. Putnam's Sons, New York, 1964.

Flood, Robert, ed. *America - God Shed His Grace On Thee*, Moody Press, Chicago, 1975.

Griffin, Bulkley S., ed. *Offbeat History*, World Publishing Company, Cleveland, 1967.

Halstead, Murat. *The Illustrious Life of William McKinley*, published by the author, 1901.

The Harpers Ferry / Boliver Eagle. Harpers Ferry, West Virginia, 1987.

Harrington, Joseph D. *Yankee Samurai: The Secret Role of Nisei in America's Pacific Victory*, Pettigrew Enterprises, Inc., Detroit, 1979.

Hickman, Norman G. *The Ultimate Quiz Book*, E.P. Dutton, Inc., New York, 1984.

Hinckley, Jack and JoAnn. *Breaking Points*, Chosen Books, Grand Rapids, Michigan, 1985.

Holman, Hamilton. *Zachary Taylor: Soldier in the White House*, Volumes I and II, Bobbs-Merrill, Indianapolis, 1951.

Hoyt, Edwin P. *William McKinley*, Reilly and Lee Company, Chicago, 1967.

Jennison, Keith W. *The Humorous Mr. Lincoln*, Bonanza Books, New York, 1965.

Kellerman, Barbara. *All the President's Kin*, The Free Press, New York, 1981.

Kirk, Elise K. *Music at the White House*, University of Illinois Press, Urbana, Illinois, 1986.

Kohlsaat, H.H. *From McKinley to Harding: Personal Recollections of Our Presidents*, Charles Scribner's Sons, New York, 1923.

Kurzeja, Wayne Samuel. *The Presidential Quotient*, Chicago Review Press, Chicago, 1984.

Leauver, Lawrence. *Make Believe: The Story of Nancy and Ronald Reagan*, Harper and Row, New York, 1983.

Mayer, Jane. *Dolley Madison*, Random House, New York, 1954.

McElroy, Richard L. *American Presidents: Fascinating Facts, Stories, and Questions of Our Chief Executives and Their Families*, Daring Books, Canton, Ohio, 1984.

McPhee, Nancy. *The Second Book of Insults*, St. Martin's Press, Inc., New York, 1981.

Nash, Bruce and Zullo, Allan. *The Baseball Hall of Shame #3*, Pocket Books, New York, 1987.

Nolan, Jeannette Covert. *The Little Giant - Stephen A. Douglas*, Julian Messner, Inc., New York, 1964.

O'Neill, Thomas P. *Man of the House*, Random House, New York, 1987.

Parents Magazine Enterprises, *The First Ladies Cook Book*, Bantam Books, Inc., New York, 1982.

Pitch, Anthony S. *Exclusively Presidential Trivia*, Mino Publications, Washington, D.C., 1985.

Reagan, Nancy. *Nancy*, Berkley Books, New York, 1980.

Sandburg, Carl. *Abraham Lincoln: The War Years*, Volume II, Dell Publishing Co., New York, 1963.

Schlossberg, Dan. *The Baseball Catalog*, Jonathan David Publishers, Inc., Middle Village, New York, 1980.

Sharp and Dunnigan Publications. *The Congressional Medal of Honor*, Sharp and Dunnigan, Forest Ranch, California, 1984.

Shepherd, Jack and Wren, Christopher. *The Almanac of Poor Richard Nixon*, World Publishing Company, Cleveland, Ohio, 1968.

Shultz, Gladys Denny. *Jenny Lind, The Swedish Nightingale*, J.B. Lippincott Co., Philadelphia, 1962.

Sievers, Harry J. *Benjamin Harrison: Hoosier President (The White House Years and After, 1884-1901)*, The Bobbs-Merrill Company, Indianapolis, 1968.

Smith, Paige. *Trial by Fire: A People's History of the Civil War and Reconstruction*, McGraw-Hill Book Company, New York, 1982.

Spear, Joseph C. *Presidents and the Press*, MIT Press, Cambridge, Massachusetts, 1984.

Spencer, Cornelia. *Straight Furrow: The Biography of Harry S Truman for Young People*, The John Day Company, New York, 1949.

Truman, Margaret. *Bess W. Truman*, Jove Books, New York, 1986.

Van Hoose, William H. *Tecumseh: An Indian Moses*, Daring Books, Canton, Ohio, 1984.

Weaver, G. S. *The Lives and Graves of Our Presidents*, Elder Publishing Company, Chicago, 1884.

Wibberly, Leonard. *The Gales of Spring: Thomas Jefferson - The Years 1789-1801*, Ariel Books, Farras, Straus, and Giroux, New York, 1965.

Witcover, Julie. *Marathon: The Pursuit of the Presidency, 1972-1976*, Viking Press, New York, 1977.

Woodward, Bob and Bernstein, Carl. *The Final Days*, Simon and Schuster, New York, 1976.

The following magazines were also used for reference: *Parade, People, National Geographic, Ohio Cues, The Buckeye Flyer, Newsweek, Saturday Evening Post*, and *Ohio Historical Society Echoes*.

Clinton's New Shoes and "Socks"

Prior to his inauguration as President in January of 1993, Bill Clinton ordered two pairs of size 13½-D shoes, costing him a total of $450. He had them specially-made by an Arkansas shoemaker. In addition, Clinton announced he would be taking black and white Socks to the White House as well. Socks is the name of the Clinton family pet cat.

At Least It's a Start

Following his election, Bill Clinton visited Washington, D.C. to meet with Congressional leaders and accept an invitation to the White House from his defeated opponent, George Bush. Later, Clinton toured the city, walking through several neighborhoods. At one point, a five year old boy tried to give him two pennies. Clinton told the boy to keep the coins and use them towards his college education!

Advice for Hillary

Barbara Bush invited Hillary Clinton to a private tour of the White House in mid-November of 1992. Barbara put her arm around Hillary, pointed to a group of reporters and warned, "Avoid *this crowd* like the plague. And if they quote you, make damn sure they heard you." Hillary responded, "That's right. I know that feeling already."